2.

THRIFT STORE

D0111046

THRIFT STORE

*Finding God's Gifts
in the Midst of the Mess*

JANE F. KNUTH

LOYOLA PRESS.
A JESUIT MINISTRY
Chicago

LOYOLA PRESS.
A JESUIT MINISTRY

3441 N. Ashland Avenue
Chicago, Illinois 60657
(800) 621-1008
www.loyolapress.com

Art credit: iStockphotography.com

Library of Congress Cataloging-in-Publication Data
Knuth, Jane.
 Thrift store graces : finding God's gifts in the midst of the mess / Jane F. Knuth.
  p. cm.
 ISBN-13: 978-0-8294-3692-1
 ISBN-10: 0-8294-3692-8
 1. Church work--United States. 2. Thrift shops--United States. 3. Charity. 4. Christian life.
I. Title.
 BV4403.K68 2012
 267'.18277417--dc23
                                                                2011046536

Printed in the United States of America.
12 13 14 15 16 17 Versa 10 9 8 7 6 5 4 3 2 1

This book is dedicated to the community of the Society of St. Vincent de Paul throughout the world.

CONTENTS

A NOTE FROM THE AUTHOR

The stories in this book are true. However, the Society of St. Vincent de Paul strictly guards the privacy of the individuals whom we help. In keeping with this practice, I changed names, occupations, physical descriptions, and details of the assistance we rendered. Any resulting resemblance to other persons is coincidental and unintentional. People's problems are rarely unique, but the gifts they gave me are—that is where the disguises may fail. I ask for forgiveness if that is the case. There are several instances where I received permission to tell a story without changes, and I am grateful for these generous souls. Some events in the book are a matter of public record. I told the story from my perspective. Other participants in the events may have differing views and memories of what occurred. I acknowledge the possibility that my memories may not coincide exactly with theirs, and I apologize for any unintended offense I may have given.

PROLOGUE:
PIECES OF STRING TOO
SMALL TO SAVE

After we die, someone else has to clean out our house. Sometimes, before we die.

Either way, it's a gift, and the gift may be accepted or rejected.

On Friday, when I walk into the St. Vincent de Paul Thrift Shop where I volunteer, there is a note on the clipboard asking if we can pick up a donation of furniture. This is not an unusual request. We have a couple of middle-aged guys (one of whom is married to me) who spend a Saturday morning every month running around town in an old Dodge truck, collecting furniture and appliances from donors and delivering the items to our customers and clients. If the items are on the heavy side, they will often enlist the help of teenagers from Hackett, the Catholic high school in town, to take the "ouch" out of the load.

Walter, our St. Vincent de Paul president, has cryptically printed in the margins of the note: "Donating everything in the apartment—bring boxes."

Someone must have died, I decide after reading it. I glance a prayer for their soul up past the ceiling and dial my husband, Dean, at work. "Can you do a pickup tomorrow? It looks like a big one—an entire apartment."

"Sure," he says. "See if you can round up a crew from Hackett High to help."

I call my contacts at the school and am delighted to learn that it is near the end of the semester and several students are desperate for volunteer hours to fulfill the required allotment for the marking period. We can use both male and female students, so I tell them to direct the teenagers who are interested to meet us at the store tomorrow morning at nine o'clock.

Next I gather some cardboard boxes and go in search of Walter.

It turns out the donation is from a friend of his, and the friend is not dead.

"Why is he giving us everything in his apartment?" I ask.

"Yeah . . . well," Walter says, shaking his head sadly, "he has cancer. Last week his doctors told him it was time to go into hospice. His son lives out of town and doesn't need much of anything, so they want to give it all to charity. My friend isn't healthy enough to do all the packing up, so be sure to send some students who can make a careful job of it, all right?"

I put several more boxes on the pile and add a stack of newspapers.

The next day I remain at the shop with some of our other volunteers, and we sort the contents of the boxes as they begin arriving. And there is a lot of that to do.

Throughout the morning, the teenagers haul in truckload after truckload of furniture and household items, along with clothing, knickknacks, and a library of books. On their second trip, they bring in a nine-foot, steel-frame, sleeper sofa that requires four of them to carry. I push things around in the back room to give them a place to put it down and say, "That's a heavy one. Did you have any trouble getting it down the stairs?"

They grunt as the front legs clunk onto the concrete floor, and then snatch their fingers out from under before they let the back feet fall. One of the young men stands upright and says, "It wouldn't go through the door, so we dropped it off the balcony." They are grinning as they slap hands all around.

"You *dropped* it?"

Dean walks in the door with two lamps in his hands, which he places next to the arms of the sofa. He says to me, "For the record, it wasn't me who caught it."

The students hoot and point at one of their buddies, who is trying to look modest in spite of his obviously macho role in the sofa escapade. He says, "I think we successfully avoided five or six catastrophes in that little maneuver."

I interrupt their guffaws. "*Seriously?* You dropped this sofa two floors and then caught it before it smashed?"

Dean flops down on the cushions looking satisfied with himself and his crew. "It was only one and a half floors.

The donor's son was a huge help. He used to play basket-ball for U of M, and he's about six foot nine and has long arms. He and Ryan stood out in the snowbank underneath the balcony, and the rest of us held on to it by our finger-nails and tipped it over the railing until they could reach up and balance the bottom edge. Then I kept my weight on the thing until the rest of the guys could run down the stairs and help them catch it."

I frown and tell them, "That could have ended very badly." Inexplicably, they all bust up laughing. Except for Dean. He is working on looking appropriately contrite.

"This is the last of the heavy furniture," he tells me, changing the subject. "The rest of the students are empty-ing all the kitchen cupboards right now. The elderly gen-tleman and his son are sitting at the kitchen table, sharing a beer, and chatting up the girls. He's really quite a charm-ing old guy—it's too bad about the cancer."

"All the kids aren't a problem, I hope."

"No, no. They're being very respectful. He's basically saying good-bye to a lifetime of possessions. It must be tough. But he seems to be enjoying telling the kids about some of the stuff. He's keeping one small suitcase to take with him to the hospice. The son is keeping a desk and a few boxfuls of memorabilia."

The students leaning on the sofa nod their heads and fill me in on some of the details. They can't quite fathom how these two men can let everything else be given away. These teenagers are only beginning to accumulate worldly goods—this glimpse into the end of the process just seems wrong to them.

"It's nice stuff," one of them says. "They could have sold it for some real money."

But the man's son is a bachelor investment banker; money isn't needed. That, too, is not possible for the teenagers to grasp. Still talking about it, they climb into the truck and head back for another load.

Meanwhile, at the shop, we sort through military records, mortgage papers, birthday cards, and owners manuals. We recycle stacks of *National Geographic*, fold monogrammed handkerchiefs, buff shoes, and pack the canned goods, rice, noodles, crackers, and Ensure into bags for the local food pantry. There is nothing we can do about the previously opened food items. Into the trash go spices, cereal, flour, sugar, eggs, and everything else from the freezer and refrigerator. I pour the liquor into the sink. The fragrance in the sorting room prompts startled looks from some of our customers, but I don't explain.

Toward the end of the day, I reach into one of the boxes and pull out an old wide-mouth peanut butter jar. There is a hand-lettered label taped on it. Inside the jar there is . . . something . . . *fuzzy*. I squint at it without opening the lid. This jar is filled to the rim with something not only fuzzy but also mildly *multicolored*. I turn it carefully in my hand, not wanting to drop it, and peer at the label. It reads:

Pieces of String Too Small to Save

I hold the jar up to the light.

Sure enough. That's exactly what it is.

That's what these stories are, too. Stories of working in a thrift store as a volunteer, attempting to do something about my estrangement from the community that surrounds me and that surrounds my church. They are stories that changed me, and because they changed me, each one is a gift.

They may be pieces of string too small to save, but I've saved them anyway. And like the gentleman who was going into hospice, I am sharing them because they have the possibility of changing someone else. But that always depends on whether the gift is accepted.

1

MARTHA AND MARY

It is 1998 and there is a woman in my parish who keeps asking me to go to Bosnia with her. Of course, I avoid this woman whenever possible. Visiting a country that has recently been ripped apart by a civil war has a certain intrigue, I'm sure, but I can think of less stressful things to do with my life. This woman's name is Martha. She is smart and organized, the mother of five, an admirable volunteer, generous with her time and money. Apparently she doesn't have enough to do to keep herself busy. It is the only reason I can think of that would compel her to organize pilgrimages to war-torn countries. In most other ways she strikes me as a down-to-earth, practical person. She reminds me of the Martha in the Bible, who efficiently hosted the Son of God and all his friends and then was chided when she asked for a little help with the dishes. I have heaps of sympathy for women like these two Marthas. They do all the work, get little credit, and ask only for a small amount of companionship in the sweltering kitchen.

Or in the war zone.

Martha makes me feel enormously guilty, which is reason enough to veer the other way whenever I see her coming.

She visits Bosnia often, and the reason is simple: Mary, the Mother of God, has reportedly been appearing there every day since 1981 to a group of six people. These people—two young men and four young women—don't just see Mary; they talk to her and she talks to them, and aside from that, all of them appear to be perfectly normal. Kind of like my fellow parishioner Martha.

This situation makes a lot of us very nervous. The reason I am one of those nervous folks is solidly faith-based: Mary, the Mother of God, has been known to appear several times in history, and she doesn't do so on a whim. Typically she is looking for some serious changes to take place among the faithful. In my Catholic upbringing and schooling, I have read about all these visitations, and I know that Mary does not mess around. She is not asking for a few more prayers, or extra coins in the offering plate. She is talking conversions, and confessions, and public displays of affection for God and all he represents. Mother Mary coming to us is not a good sign. It is like having the greatest lawyer in the world come to your house to offer you legal advice. Wonderful to have such excellent help, but it is also a sign of calamity.

If I go to Bosnia, as Martha thinks I should, there are going to be consequences. There may have to be a deeper relationship between me and Mary, one that requires something from me, and I'm not sure I'm ready for that.

I like my life the way it is. I am happily married, the mother of two school-age daughters, a part-time teacher, and a volunteer at a St. Vincent de Paul Thrift Store. I go to church every Sunday. I talk to God the Father, Jesus, Joseph, and Mary on a regular schedule, and they nod back. Plus, the Holy Spirit and I wave to each other occasionally. There is plenty to fill my time in all of that, and surely Mary, the Mother of God, does not want me to interrupt my activities and go halfway across the globe to some town in the hills of Bosnia called Medjugorje. Besides, I have a conviction that I should avoid going to places with names I can't pronounce and a language I don't speak.

Martha owns a persistent faith, however. She plans the trip, preorders plane tickets and hotel reservations, and keeps me informed about the arrangements for me and all the other people she has convinced to go with us. I politely smile and shake my head at her as I go in the other direction. I tell my husband, Dean, how foolish Martha is, because the United Nations is threatening to run bombing raids in Kosovo. This war is not over by a long shot. "Besides," I say to him, "we don't have the money." He nods and seems to agree with me.

Three months later, our tax refund comes in the mail. It is the exact amount needed for Martha's pilgrimage to Medjugorje. I mention this coincidence to my faithful Lutheran husband, and he says, "We have no burning plans for the money. Go if you want to."

2

ANOTHER MARY

The next time I volunteer at the St. Vincent de Paul Thrift Store, I am arranging the religious articles in the display cabinets while my fellow volunteer, Mary Vrbancic, runs the cash register. Our store is a small, concrete-block structure situated on the back edge of everything. There are two abandoned houses next door, a homeless shelter across the street, and railroad tracks half a block away. The bell tower of St. Augustine Cathedral is within earshot, but it clearly faces the opposite direction—the direction of traffic flow and a bustling downtown. On the other side of the block, the St. Vincent de Paul shop is strategically gazing into the impoverished neighborhood. This is good. This is where we want to be.

Our merchandise reflects everything that any retailer sells, but usually appears on our shelves a few years later. We sort and price what our donors bring to us, arrange the items in attractive displays, and depend on our neighborhood customers to turn it into part of God's plan to save our living souls.

According to the Rule of the St. Vincent de Paul Society (our spiritual guidelines), we are always the students, and the people we help are always the teachers. Our job is to pray, listen, clothe, feed, comfort, and assist in whatever way our neighbors need most. Our neighbors' job is to help us recognize God's homely face and to teach us his ways. This is such ridiculous religious thinking that I fell in love with it.

When I first started volunteering at St. Vincent de Paul, there were nine elderly ladies who ran the place: Dorothy, Mary, Virginia, Alice, Rosemary, Catherine, Bernie D., Bernie B., and another one whose name I can't remember.

Mary is the mentor I need most right now. Mary is white-haired and quick-witted, suffers fools not at all, and is of Croatian stock.

I look up from the holy cards I am sorting and casually tell her I have made plans to visit Bosnia-Herzegovina.

"Why the hell would you do that?" she says curiously. Mary's language can be prickly, but her tone of voice seldom is.

I tell her about the Virgin Mary appearing and my friend Martha's habit of taking innocent people on pilgrimages, and Mary says, "Sounds like a crazy thing to do. But Medjugorje would be one thing I'd really like to see—I talk to Our Lady every night."

"Have you ever been to the former Yugoslavia?" I ask her.

"Sure, years ago, when things were stable. No one speaks English in the whole damn country, and I never ate so much cabbage in my life. It was a pretty place before everybody went crazy and started shooting each other. All my family is from there. My mother came over here to marry a friend of her uncle's, but when she arrived in the United States and met the fellow, she didn't like him. Her uncle was angry because the friend had paid her passage, but she wouldn't have anything to do with him, and there was a big spat. One of her uncle's other friends from Croatia was there at the time, and he thought it was pretty funny, so he said to my mom, 'If you won't marry him, will you marry me?'"

My mother looked him over and said, "Yeah, I will.' So he paid the first guy for her passage, and my parents were married for forty years."

I love Mary's stories, so I keep her going. "Where did you stay in Croatia when you visited?"

"My cousins live in a little village—a *selo*. They took me sightseeing through castles and caverns and all the churches around. Yesterday I got a call from one of them, but in the middle of the conversation I forgot a word." She shakes her head sadly. "No one is left here to speak Croatian with anymore, so I'm out of practice."

My interest intensifies, and I ask, "You speak Croatian?"

"Of course I do. It's just *selo* Croatian—the kind they speak in the villages, but that's fine for what I need to say."

The language barrier is the main thing that has me worried . . . aside from the bullets and fifty-millimeter shells, of course. So I ask her if she would be willing to teach me a few words and phrases of Croatian.

"Sure, honey, I'll be glad to. Here's a pencil—you better get started."

Dorothy walks by and hears me butchering "Dobar dan." I tell her about my trip, and she asks me to bring her a rosary from Medjugorje. "We sell rosaries here in the store," I point out.

"Yes, but I think it would be nice to have one that was blessed by Mary."

"She does that?" I say in surprise.

Dorothy nods. "It shouldn't be a problem. Rosaries are a big thing with her."

When the other volunteers hear that I am jetting off to Europe, they think that I am taking a vacation. I don't try to straighten them out. I realize this is odd behavior on my part. I volunteer at a faith-based charity with people who share my religious convictions, and although the ongoing apparitions in Medjugorje are not officially sanctioned by the Catholic Church, they are not condemned either.

At this moment, most of the official Catholics don't have much to say about it one way or the other. It's one of those wait-and-see strategies that helps them stay clear from making major theological commitments when people are paying attention. We Catholics are much more adept at talking about people and events after everything and everyone involved has died away. Officially, for example, there is no such thing as a "living saint."

So as far as the faithful can tell, where Medjugorje is concerned, for now we are on our own. If we want to go there, fine. If we prefer to ignore it, that's okay with Rome too.

The problem with this kind of benign neglect is that it forces a person like me to actually make a move based solely on . . . well . . . *faith*. If the Church would make a pronouncement one way or the other, then I would have the choice to either rebel or obey. The way it stands, I have to decide either to ignore the reports of Mary's appearances and her words or I have to pay attention. In my case, it's one of those uncomfortable moments of "I believe, Lord. Help my unbelief!"

Back at the thrift shop, Mary Vrbancic teaches me to say, "Good day," "I'm sorry," "How much is the bill?" "This is delicious," "Where are the restrooms?" and "No cabbage, please."

3

I Don't Remember
Asking for This

I live in great fear that God will decide one day to hit me over the head with one of his so-called gifts in order to get my attention. I think that day may have arrived. I have been interviewing people all day in the small office at the St. Vincent de Paul Thrift Shop. We are attempting to defeat some of the gloom in our town by helping to pay bills to prevent evictions or the shutoff of utilities and by giving our neighbors clothing, furniture, and whatever else they identify as the need in their lives that is crying out the loudest. But we are not trying to save them from all their misfortunes; that would not be possible. The manual of the Society of St. Vincent de Paul (our operating instructions), specifically states that "we are not fanatics."

I do not say we should go out indiscriminately and take on everything, but rather those things God lets us know He wants of us.

—St. Vincent de Paul

And so, in a nonfanatical way, I am sitting at a desk, listening to people tell me about their troubles, and promising them whatever help we are able to provide.

First thing in the morning, a young mother comes in who has been trying to catch up on her heating bill since last winter and is still losing ground. It is September, and she is five hundred dollars behind, with cool temperatures looming just around the bend. After I help her, I meet a middle-aged couple who have jobs and a realistic budget, but medical bills are sinking their ship bit by bit. She has back problems and he has asthma. The copays and occasional hospitalizations have eaten up their retirement money and sapped their optimism. Neither of them wants to ask for help, but neither wants the electricity turned off either. I listen to a nineteen-year-old whose mother is kicking her out of the house because she is pregnant with her second out-of-wedlock child. This girl is not even aware of how hard her next few months are going to be. I put her in contact with a crisis pregnancy center that might be able to find an apartment for her to share with another teenage mom who is working with their agency. Not the best solution, but not the worst either.

The names and faces of the people begin to blur together around one-thirty. I get a phone message to call "Angela." *Which one was she? The one who asked for rental assistance, or did she have the new baby who needed a crib? Maybe she was the CNA at the nursing home?* I look up her file, call her number, and gradually remember our conversation from only a couple of hours ago.

After all the clients have departed and my coworkers have cashed-out the register, I am still on hold with the electric company, attempting to make a pledge on someone's bill. When I finally get through, everyone has left except Peggy. She pokes her head in the office door and asks if I am about ready to go out to the parking lot with her.

I file the last client record and reach in the back of the desk drawer for my purse, which I loop over my shoulder. I stand up from the desk, and I know already that something isn't right. The purse is too floppy and noticeably underweight. I take it off my shoulder and look inside.

No wallet.

I look in the bottom of the drawer to see if my wallet has fallen out. Empty.

I paw through the tissues and old receipts in the bottom of the purse. No wallet hiding under any of that. I zip open the side pocket.

No wallet and . . . *no cell phone, either.*

Peggy is watching all this and guesses at what it means. "Have you lost your keys?"

I start to shake my head, but then I look in the skinny purse again.

I grab my coat off the back of the chair, stick a frantic hand in the right-side pocket, and pull out a ring of keys.

Peggy says, "Good, you found them."

"Yes . . ."

People panic in different ways. For me, panic is not a heart-pounding, fight-or-flight response to disaster. In my case, panic seems to be more like an irrational conclusion that everything is more than likely just fine, *even though it appears terribly wrong.*

I say to Peggy as I put on my coat. "My wallet isn't in my purse. I hope I left it at home."

She stops buttoning her jacket. "Your wallet is missing?"

I close one eye at her rephrasing but say calmly. "Probably not. Like I said, it might be at home."

Peggy has not panicked. It's not Peggy's wallet and cell phone that are missing after all. She has a very concerned look on her face as she says to me, "I'll go out and look in the Dumpster, just in case. Sometimes, after a thief removes the cash, they will throw the wallet in the nearest trash can."

"It might not be missing. I forget things at home a lot," I repeat.

Peggy raises one eyebrow and says, "Let's ask St. Anthony for some help." We do that and then she tells me to go look out front in the street gutter while she checks the Dumpster.

After we fail to find the wallet in all the trash receptacles on the property, do I call the police? No. I continue to insist that I have likely been foolish and left both my cell phone and my wallet in my house. I then foolishly drive home and discover I have been fooling myself.

So that is why I call the police a full thirty minutes after I have discovered the theft. They, of course, tell me to drive back downtown to the place where the theft took place. Now it is an hour since my wallet came up missing. The policeman is an extremely nice person who tells me twice I have "not been stupid." After he gets all the names of the people I interviewed in the office during the day, plus their addresses and Social Security numbers, he gives me a little yellow card with a case number on it and tells me to begin calling all the credit card companies and the banks to cancel everything in my financial life. But all that information is at home, so I get back in my car and drive there. Again.

As I drive away, I see the policeman at the side of the building, peering into our Dumpster with a flash light.

It is five-thirty Friday evening, the classic moment in the week when I most desire to put up my feet at home and sip on a beer.

Instead, I spend two hours calling 1-800 numbers and speaking with some well-trained bank-security zealots. When I tell them that I have been robbed, they all say things like, "I'm so sorry this happened to you. If you are able to give us some basic information, we'll cancel your cards straightaway." I don't have certain basic information, however, like the multidigit numbers on the cards, so I call Dean at work, and he reads the numbers off his cards. This is logical. We have joint accounts; the bills come to our joint address; we have the same last name and pay one bill. I call the zealots again and tell them I have lost my cards but Dean still has his. They cancel everything anyway, his and mine. Apparently, this is necessary.

Tomorrow is the annual celebration of the Feast of St. Vincent de Paul. Eighty Vincentians from all over the diocese are coming to our parish for Mass and a catered dinner, and I am in charge of the dinner. I have no driver's license, no ATM cards, no credit cards, no cash, and an empty gas tank. What's more, there is not a single bottle of beer in my refrigerator.

4

ACCEPTING THE GIFT

I spend the next twenty-four hours frustrated and hot; those two things always seem to go together. For the weekend feast-day celebrations my mom loans me money, graciously chauffeurs me around, and lets me borrow her cell phone. *How do theft victims cope who don't have family resources like mine?*

At least it is an educational experience, and for me as a teacher, educational experiences are deemed valuable no matter how painful. I learn a little about the legal system, a little about the banking system, a little about retail loss prevention, and I develop an authentic interest in situational ethics.

While canceling one of my credit cards by phone, I learn the card has been used three times within an hour at three different stores for purchases totaling over a thousand dollars. I call the kind Kalamazoo police officer who took all the information at the crime scene. He tells me that because the credit cards were used in Portage, the suburb south of Kalamazoo, this is now a different crime, and I need to call the Portage police to report it. As far as the law goes, it is eye-opening to discover that, if possible, one should avoid being robbed by a thief who is so inconsiderate as to use the stolen credit cards in a jurisdiction different from the one where the robbery took place.

I call the Portage police, and they ask for the precise addresses where the credit cards were used. I call the bank back and find out they don't know exactly. They have the names of the stores on their computers but not the addresses. There are three possible Walgreens, two possible Meijers, and two Wal-Marts to choose amongst. The bank will not be able to discern these addresses until after the charges come through the following week. I will need to call them back then. After that, I will need to call the police and give them the information, because the bank is not allowed to talk to the police about my accounts.

I repeat this process with all three credit cards. Everyone wants me to drive to their bank location and sign paperwork before they will release anything to me. The bank clerks are helpful about making multiple copies, the police are patient, and all of this steals lots of my time and petroleum. I don't tell the police I am driving all over town without a driver's license, because there is enough crime in our town for them to worry about already.

I ask one banker, "Who loses the money? I'm protected because I reported the theft, so who takes the hit? The stores?"

He shakes his head grimly. "No. The way the laws are written we take the loss, and it's very frustrating, because if the stores had checked ID, the perpetrators couldn't have used your cards. But with the swipe pads, they don't bother. Asking for ID slows things up at the checkout and annoys some customers, and since the stores won't lose the money, they have little incentive to change the way they do business."

I tell the banker about all the running around I have to do, and all the phone calls, and he nods. "A lot of people don't bother to do what you're doing because it's not their loss either. But if you don't do it, we can't give the police the information from your account, and the thief will never be caught."

I think about this while I am driving around visiting bankers and police departments. How many people would actually do what I am doing?

Come to think of it, why am I doing what I am doing?

The thief who stole my wallet was someone who needed financial help, or they wouldn't have been in the St. Vincent de Paul shop, sitting in the office, telling me their troubles. They must have been feeling pretty desperate to filch the wallet and the cell phone in the mere minutes they were allowed to be alone in the room. The sympathy I felt all day for these people hasn't just disappeared. I feel a vague sense of disappointment that I didn't help them enough to prevent the impulse to steal from me. I feel no rage, not even disgust. It's more like sadness. This person who stole my things is not only a poor person; they are now a poor person who is wanted by the law. Since meeting me, their burdens have expanded immeasurably.

On the upside, the thief must have had a giddy time spending thousands of dollars in a little under two hours at seven different stores. I picture them flinging merchandise from the shelves into the carts, waiting excitedly in the checkout lines, loading the sacks into the car, and speeding off to the next crime scene.

What a rush.

Then I picture myself, the victim. I have lost approximately $200 because I had just cashed a check. I will have to replace my cell phone and buy minutes, which will be another $150. The replacement wallet won't be free either. I lost a couple of gift cards that people had given me but I hadn't used yet. Someday I will have to order a new library card and new insurance cards. This is all a nuisance, but more troubling is the fact that the thief knows not only my name but also where I volunteer each week and where I live. And since I am in the phone book, add my home phone number to that.

On my way to the next bank, when I glance in the rearview mirror, I notice that smack between my eyebrows I am developing one of those vertical worry lines I so often see etched on the faces of people who come into St. Vincent de Paul.

Is it worth it to pursue justice? Wouldn't it be easier to be the noble Christian, just offer it all up as a sacrifice to God and forgive the thief with the hopes of meeting someday in paradise, where we can laugh it all off? I'm not feeling a particular need for vengeance, so why not just forgive and forget and leave justice in God's hands, where he likes it? I think about it for a few minutes but keep driving to the banks.

My thoughts run something like this: I'm a teacher by profession, but I'm also a good student. I have always been a good student. My philosophy is that there is something to be learned in every one of life's events, good or bad. The most telling characteristics of good students are that they show up, do the work, and turn everything in on time. I decide I will share my predicament with my fellow Vincentians so I can garner their advice. But now I have to make a decision about what to do next.

I think about my personal reference material for ethical situations like this one: The Bible. I begin a mental search. I come upon "an eye for an eye," but that doesn't really fit the case. I will not miss the money all that much because I have sitting in the bank many times what I lost. The thief could spend an inordinate number of years trying to pay it all back, which doesn't really feel like fair retribution.

I move on and come upon forgiving "seven times seventy," and "turn the other cheek," which don't quite fit the situation either, since I'm not likely to be robbed that many times, nor have I been physically assaulted. My personal morality dilemma is more about whether as a member of the St. Vincent de Paul Society—namely, "a friend of the poor," I should pursue this thief. And whether the justice that the legal system will lay down will actually result in what I desire as a merciful Christian. Do I want this person, who originally came to us in need, to go to jail? If so, for how long? If I let it all go, forgive the person in my heart, and move on, am I leaving some other person vulnerable to being robbed next week?

In the end, the biblical moral question feels most like "Am I my brother's keeper?" And the answer muddling around in my brain is, *You betcha, whether my brother likes it or not.*

So, having reached that conclusion, as a good student, I prevail upon myself to read the brochures the policeman gave me from the Crime Victim Advocacy Program. I take notes from every conversation with the bankers and the police, and I turn in all the information I gather, in duplicate, to both departments. The police and the bankers are delighted.

Criminals ought to avoid robbing good students.

5

TALL MARY

She stands on a glass shelf display in the middle of the room, directly in the line of sight from the front entrance. We all have to work around her. She is the biggest Mary in the place, made of painted chalk composition and twenty-four inches tall, counting the base with the snake. This is the classic *Our Lady of Grace*, which is the pose Mary chose for herself when she instructed Catherine Labouré in nineteenth-century France to have a medal struck, the one that quickly became known as the Miraculous Medal. Mary wears a white ankle-length dress, blue belted in an Empire waist, and draped in a deeper blue mantle. Her hands are down and spread palms out. She stands on a half-globe, a hissing, writhing snake daintily pressed under her instep.

She looks worried, but not in a neurotic way. More of a concerned empathy directed slightly downward, as if she is watching small children who have eaten too many sweets and are feeling it.

Mary Kay, one of our volunteers, calls her our "make-an-offer-Mary" because she resides over the used rosaries and crucifixes that we let people take away for a donation.

When I come in to work my volunteer shift at the store the next week, Mary Kay and Pat are standing at the cash register. Their eyes shift toward the clock when I walk in, to check how late I am this time. They are both former third-grade teachers, so I hear "a diller, a dollar, a ten o'clock scholar" quite often, but I do remember to always wipe my feet on the mat. Today when I look up from my feet, I know something is missing in the store. It takes only a moment for me to figure it out.

"Where's our tall Mary?" I immediately ask.

"Don't you start, too," Pat says.

"What happened?" I demand.

"Nothing happened. We sold her. A customer wanted to buy her, so we wrapped her up and off she went."

"Aw . . . really?"

Mary Kay gives me a sympathetic look. "Kind of a shock, isn't it? She's been standing there so many years, I guess we all forgot she had a price tag on her."

"Are we going to get another one soon?"

"Elizabeth has been looking through the catalogs, but she says all the statues available to ship immediately are uglier than sin. She can't find one she likes that isn't on back-order. There's no telling when we'll get our new Mary." Elizabeth, one of our volunteers, has the job of purchasing the religious articles, books, and gifts that we sell in the store as an additional part of our fund-raising.

"Aw . . . ," I say again. This does not feel good to me. This is the exact wrong time to be without a tall Mary statue in the store looking over things. I have not realized how comforting it is to have her pinning that snake to the earth with her toes while we do our work. I am unsettled by last week's theft, uneasy about how I should be reacting as "a friend of the poor," and irritated that the replacement statue may not be available quickly.

Seeing my disappointment and misinterpreting it, Mary Kay says, "Maybe we shouldn't have sold her. You're not the only one who is upset."

Pat sighs. "It was a statue. We are a charity. The money went to help some poor people, which is what we are supposed to be doing. Everyone needs to get a grip."

"Oh, absolutely," I agree. "We've had other Mary statues in the past and sold them. It's just that I've had a stressful week, and. . . . " I tell them about the whole wallet event and warn them to lock up their purses, and they exclaim and obvious questions arise as to why I had not locked mine securely.

I compulsively repeat this conversation several times during the coming week, which fails to calm me in any way at all. So I resort to praying a lot of extra rosaries, too. The Blessed Virgin Mary and I have been prayer partners for most of my adult life. The classic prayer, the Hail Mary, which we Catholics say to her, is a combination of Scripture passages and a weensy bit of morbidity.

Hail Mary, full of grace.
The Lord is with you.
Blessed art thou among women,
and blessed is the fruit of thy womb, Jesus.
Holy Mary, Mother of God,
pray for us sinners,
now and at the hour of our death. Amen.

This is a spot-on prayer in many ways. For one, it's all about a woman and her relationship with God and her relationship with other women. The opening lines come from the angel Gabriel, an obvious admirer, who doesn't mince words about where Mary stands with the Almighty. She is not only *full of grace*; Mary is *with the Lord*. And Gabriel also points out that she is simultaneously *among women,* almost like she's a member of a women's sodality, or circle, or those groups that call themselves daughters or guilds. Right out of the gate Mary comes across like the mother of all church ladies in this prayer.

Next up, we delicately mention pregnancy. There are not many prayers I know of that do this. Sure, in the creed we say that Jesus is "conceived by the Holy Spirit and born of the Virgin Mary," but that skips over the nine months way too quickly. Any woman who has gone through pregnancy can appreciate the reference to "fruit" and how slowly it grows and ripens over the better part of a year. Elizabeth, John the Baptist's mother, gave us this line. She had gone through the whole infertility thing and the surprise pregnancy to boot, so who better to speak for us than she?

And who better to speak *up* for us than the Mother of God, herself? A priest once explained in a homily that the reason we Catholics talk to Mary a lot is precisely because she is Jesus' mother. "Think of it this way," I remember the priest saying. "If you smash up your dad's car, how are you going to break the news to him? First you go to your mom and explain the whole accident to her—why you were driving a little fast and how you intend to pay for the damages, and maybe you ask her what kind of day Dad had at work. Exactly the same thing with God. It makes total sense in dicey situations that people would go to Mary and see if she will put in a good word. Might not help, but it certainly can't hurt."

Last, we have the morbid bit: *Pray for us sinners, now and at the hour of our death. Amen.* We focus on nonspecific flaws and death. This type of talk is necessary for relationships between women. Our true friends are not the people we party with. Nor are they necessarily our neighbors, coworkers, people we talk to on Facebook, or even our shopping buddies. They are not always the people we help either. More often, a mark of a true friend is someone who knows all our problem areas, and we still dare to ask her for help in a crisis.

Like death for instance.

Or like when we have been robbed and we don't know who did it, but we know we spent at least thirty minutes giving the thief sympathy and promising them money.

I get out my rosary and work those beads pretty hard. It helps with the fixation more than I expect.

6

BUY ONE, GET ONE FREE

It is a rainy fall day, and a young boy, perhaps ten years old, tugs his way through the door of the thrift store. The plate glass is heavy, and the handle about six inches too high above his shoulder for good purchase, but he manages to catch the weight of it with his bony elbow and wedges his way through until he stands dripping on our laminate floor.

He shakes the water out of his hair and eyes, sneezes a couple of times, and after swiping at his nose, surveys his new, dry surroundings. His eyes brighten with curiosity and possibilities as he takes in the multitude of cast-off goods that line the shelves of our display floor.

From behind the cash register, we in turn survey him.

No adult follows after him. We peer hopefully past him through the foggy glass, but not another soul appears.

Uh-oh, I say to myself, *another loose one.*

As a teacher I have a fondness for bright, curious children—as long as they are supervised. But rainy days tend to bring in the neighborhood children as if our tiny store is the local substitute for an enclosed mall.

Sometimes boys his age will march boldly up to us and offer to hire themselves out as day laborers. Do we need our leaves raked? Will we pay them to take out our trash? Do we give away free things?

And sometimes, boys his age will slide around in the back aisles, send furtive glances our way, and walk out with bulging pockets. I am not typically troubled by juvenile peccadilloes. If I suspect that young children are up to no good, I engage them in conversation and alarm them with attention.

I might say something like, "I think I know your mom. Doesn't she shop in here a lot?"

I brace myself, but this young man is too busy browsing the merchandise to notice us. He starts on the left wall and works his way slowly around the room, checking out every rack, as if used clothing, knick-knackery, and pre-owned linens are the most interesting things he has seen all year. Suspicion begins to fill me up, and I don't like the feeling. Generally I trust people, unless given ample evidence to the contrary, but now I am not in a trusting mood. I have talked with too many cynical bankers and filled out too many theft reports. It is all messing with my attitude in a negative way. Today I am too busy to keep a constant watch on this young boy or to strike up a conversation, but his presence in the store weighs on my thoughts.

Half an hour passes before he approaches the checkout counter with three shirts just his size.

Does he know these cost money? We wonder.

He does, and he counts out the needed four dollars in coins, plus tax.

Our cashier, Dottie, rings up the sale, bags his purchase, and says, "You know, there's a sale today—buy one, get one free. You can pick out three more shirts if you like." He flashes a delighted smile and returns to the sales floor. But this time he brings back two shirts that are much too big for him. When our volunteer Joan points out the problem, he replies: "Oh, these are for my dad—he needs some new clothes too."

I shake myself mentally and wonder how much damage can be done to a person by being a victim of crime. Many of our clients, because of the neighborhoods they live in, have more than likely been crime victims many times in their lives. But they are not all filled with suspicion and dread. There is a lesson for me here, but I pray that it will not be too costly.

Buy one get one free would be nice.

I decide I need a break. No, not just a break. I need to be coddled. I call up my hair dresser, Nan, and make an appointment.

When I arrive and settle into her comfy chair, Nan tells me that she is *not* in the business of making people beautiful. She is in the business of helping people feel better about themselves. She knows that if customers leave the shop feeling unattractive or uninteresting, they won't be back. Each time I sit down in her chair, she questions me carefully about how short I want my hair cut, even though she has been cutting it for twenty-six years. She asks after my daughters and my husband as she brings the water to a comforting temperature. She massages my scalp with her fingers and protects my clothing from drips.

She is aware that in giving me a haircut, she is also giving me a bit of love. I soak up her love for an hour and afterward, perfumed and pampered, I drive back to the store.

The St. Vincent de Paul Society is something like a beauty salon.

Each morning, when we volunteers gather in a circle to pray, one of the requests we regularly make is that "everyone who walks through our door will know God loves them." How they will figure this out is God's business. We are only expressing our awareness that *our* job is to be the tool that God uses.

When I return to the store with newly trimmed hair and a fresh attitude, a gentleman is waiting to see me to ask for help with his rent. We helped him the previous month. With regret, I tell him we can't do the same for him again so soon. He is not offended. Far from it. He hadn't really expected us to help him twice in a row, but he doesn't know where else to go. When I apologize for turning him down, he apologizes for asking.

He says, "I appreciated the way you treated me before, and I feel foolish being back here, but I knew you would treat me well again, whether you could help or not."

In other words; he has felt the love.

I give him information on how to get help from the next nearest St. Vincent de Paul Society at St. Catherine Parish in Portage. He is grateful even though it means another day, another bus ride, and another wait in line.

Although I haven't helped the man, he has helped me. Something else was stolen from me along with my wallet. Nan and this grateful man have given me my groove back.

The next day I am not a volunteer, but I am still a student. It is the day for my weekly oil-painting class, one of my favorite afternoons in the week.

My oil-painting teacher, Ken Freed, is a master painter, but he is also an excellent teacher, which is a rare combination. He teaches us about composition, color theory, the care and feeding of brushes, and where to buy the best paint. He knows how to give suggestions that improve the entire painting, and he has no scruples about taking the brush out of our hands and demonstrating what he wants to teach. Amid this wealth of knowledge he has one instruction that overrides everything else he teaches. *Oil painting is supposed to be fun*, he repeatedly tells us. It is challenging and frustrating; it requires patience and planning; there is endless reworking; and the finished product is never perfect. None of that, however, should prevent us from having fun. In fact, if we're not having fun, then we probably won't keep painting long enough to produce something worth framing.

Today in the class, I am standing in front of my painting chewing on my lip. It is an overly ambitious scene consisting of five children and their grandmother. This is way above my amateur level but not boring, which is why I have kept at this same painting for over a year. At this moment, it appears something has gone terribly wrong in the perspective of Grandma's hand, and two of the children are cross-eyed. Usually these problems would make for an interesting afternoon, but I am not dealing with it today. Instead, I am grimacing and choking up on the brush.

Without comment, Ken observes me wipe off fifteen dollars' worth of cobalt blue with a Bounty paper towel. I toss the wadded towel onto the pallet and say, "Her hand looks like a paw, and I can't seem to make it right no matter what I try. What am I doing wrong?"

He squints at the painting for a few minutes and then drawls, "You're not having fun. That's what you're doing wrong."

I scowl at the canvas. "That's because I can't get the silly fingers right."

He lets that sit in the air for half a minute while he picks up a brush that is three times the size of the one I am using. He dips it into the paint. "No, that's not your problem at all," he says, concentrating on the shadows in the background near Grandma's hand. "Painting is supposed to be fun. If you're not having fun, then you're not doing it right. It doesn't matter if you put eight fingers on each hand, as long as you're enjoying yourself. That's what oil painting is about. *That* alone is the purpose. Getting the hand perfect has nothing to do with it." He takes about five strokes and returns the brush back to me. "As soon as you loosen up and start to enjoy yourself—trust me—that hand will work itself out."

Ken, in his spiritual artiness, has given me the gift I need most right now. The gift of the stolen wallet may have been pricey, but at least this gift is free.

Maybe Christianity is something like oil painting: if we're not feeling the joy at least occasionally, then we're probably not doing it right.

The *Rule of the International Confederation of the Society of St. Vincent de Paul*, section 1.7 tells us: "Vincentians pray that the Holy Spirit may guide them during their visits and make them channels for the peace and joy of Christ."

The job of being a Christian is challenging and frustrating. It requires patience and planning; there is endless reworking, and the finished product is never perfect. And even though it won't be fun every minute, overall if we can channel peace and joy, then we hope that means we're doing it right.

I am thinking that instead of choking up on the brush, maybe I need to grip a wider one in my hand and work on the background for a while.

7

A Gift with Operating Instructions

Through no effort of my own, seven days pass in turmoil and frustration. I'm not one of those people who turns things over to God and lets him keep them. I tend to grab them back and chew on them every few minutes. Then I say, "Okay God, I'm putting this in your hands. But I want to see an outline and first draft by Wednesday so I know you're working on it."

It is exactly one week after the theft, and I am sitting in the office at St. Vincent de Paul with Judy, another volunteer. We are interviewing a young mother who has a shutoff notice on her utility bill. She is only one month behind, and the bill is manageable, so I pull out a pen and begin. While I am filling out the paperwork, I ask her how she finds herself in this predicament, and she sighs and tells me the money she had put aside for the bill was stolen.

I stop writing and look at her.

She is sitting quietly, sadness in her eyes, telling us she has experienced the same thing I have experienced— this thing that has me alternately clenching my jaw and doing intentional breathing. Her unnatural calm deeply impresses me. Judy and I share a look.

"What do you mean it was stolen?" I say. "How did that happen?"

She sighs and replies, "It's a long story."

"Would you tell us?"

"Okay. Well, my husband needed heart surgery, and I had to take him to Ann Arbor for it. For the week I was gone, I left my two kids with my friend, and I gave her the money to pay the utility bill. I thought she had paid it until I got the shutoff notice yesterday. When I went to her, she told me she had spent it instead. So now I'm behind, and they want to shut my heat off."

Judy says, "And you have a sick husband. . . ."

She smiles slightly. "Yes, but he's doing better every day."

"And this was your friend, who did this to you?" I ask.

She shrugs her shoulders, and the sadness comes back.

I look at Judy, and we both shake our heads. I tell this young mother we will help take care of the bill and that she shouldn't worry about it. Then I explain that, as members of the St. Vincent de Paul Society, we see the people we help as our spiritual teachers and ourselves as students. I say, "I need to tell you, I was robbed last week, and I'm not handling it nearly as well as you are. You have a sick husband and a bill you can't pay, and the person who did this is the same person you trusted to watch over your children."

Her eyes widen. She nods but doesn't say anything.

I continue, "I was robbed by a stranger, I can pay all my bills, and I don't have a sick husband, but I've been bothered over this thing all week. May I ask you to tell me how you are handling this so well? Would you be willing to share your advice?"

She draws back and looks at me skeptically. "You really want to know?"

I pick up a pen and open a pad of paper. "Yes, I really want to know. In fact, I'm going to write it down."

She smiles uncertainly and cocks her head. "Okay then," she says slowly. "The first thing you do is you pray about it."

I write a number one and next to it put *pray*. "Okay, that's fine. I've been doing that. What's next?"

She holds out the palms of her hands and lifts them up. "Then you release it. If you keep it inside, it will only hurt you. You've got to release it to God and let it go."

I nod and write. "I'm working on that. Not there yet, but I'm trying. What else?"

She is enjoying being the teacher. She smiles at me and says, "After that, you tell the truth."

I stop writing and look at her intently. *Does this woman know I'm a bit of a storyteller?*

She nods and says, "Don't hold anything back. Tell exactly what happened, and don't exaggerate. Just tell the truth."

I write it. "Okay. Anything else?"

Now her face becomes solemn. "One last thing—and this is important: don't try to save that person. That's not your job."

I am holding my breath.

"God saves people," she tells me seriously. "That's his job, not yours."

God saves people, I repeat to myself, after she leaves. *I don't save people.* My job is to comfort, clothe, listen, and help pay a few bills. I give out hugs, prayers, and money, not salvation from sins.

This feels like serious instruction, and I am paying serious attention.

It is one of those moments when the curtain between heaven and earth feels thinner than usual.

8

PART OF THE COMMUNITY

After volunteering at the store on Eleanor Street for several years, I feel like an old-timer. But that would be an exaggeration in the St. Vinnie's world where Dorothy, Bernie D., Alice, and Mary have served a combined total of one hundred years. We've got snapshots of them in beehive hairdos. They were members when the tornado of 1980 took the back off the building as it skipped over the city. These ladies have been around longer than all four bishops of the diocese and have given each of these men proportionate advice too.

One day, the four women are pricing clothes and chatting about all the time that has gone past. The conversation wanders off into the everydayness of arthritis and dissident digestions. "Something always hurts," Mary says matter-of-factly. "There isn't a way to sit or stand or lean that doesn't make some part of me ache."

Bernie grimaces and comments to no one in particular, "It sure would be nice to be young again." They all nod and keep sorting clothing.

Dorothy says, "But not too young. I wouldn't want to be a teenager again in a million years."

"Heavens, no," Bernie says, and everyone concurs. The sounds of the pricing guns click for several seconds more, and then she admits, "I guess I wouldn't want to be in my twenties either—too many important decisions to make."

"You're right," Alice says. "What to do for a living, where to live, who to marry, when to start a family, when to buy a house, which bills to pay when—that was a stressful decade." They are all nodding.

Now I am getting into the game. "How about your thirties?" I ask. "Would you do that again?"

They all look at me and then look at each other, narrowing their eyes in thought. Dorothy speaks first. "I guess not. My thirties decade was way too much work: babies, diapers, chasing toddlers, fixing up the house, and then all the volunteer work they want you to do at the kids' schools and church."

Bernie says, "Besides that, the men were working hard building their careers and were never home. I'm lucky I survived it with my sanity intact."

So far, I am on the same page with my coworkers. Their summations of the decades in a woman's life echo my own. This surprises me. These ladies are all thirty to forty years my senior, but apparently their lives followed a basic pattern similar to mine. I've never been one of those who thought high school was a high point of existence. I had some fun with sports, friends, and school, but a lot of what I remember involves excruciating social lessons that I would never wish to repeat. Their assessment of the twenties decade fits mine too: college major, graduate school, where to live, job hunting, and the enormous marriage-

and-babies decisions. All of it exciting but not something that needs repeating. And they are right about the thirties, too—I never worked so hard in my life. There are years in that decade I can't even remember.

I am waiting now for their opinion of the forties decade, where I reside at this moment.

It is the end of the day, and they are removing their aprons and putting away the pricing equipment on the cart. The phone rings, and they wave their hands at it, in a mutual decision to let the answering machine pick it up. Everyone is searching for stashed purses and buttoning coats, leaving me hanging in the wind of their memories, so I speak up. "What about your forties? Would you want to be that age again?"

They don't even stop to think about it, as if it's a given. "Oh, yes," Bernie says. "Forty is the best part of being young. The big decisions are made, the work slows a bit by then, and you've been through most of the parenting stages at least once."

Dorothy smiles, "And the aches and pains haven't begun to bear down yet. There aren't so many funerals, either. I'd do the forties again in a minute."

Mary notices something in my face and laughs. "Don't look now, sweetie. You're in the middle of the good old days. Better enjoy it."

I realize this is an amazing gift I have just received. My fellow volunteers have given me a glimpse of *now*. Now is a blurry thing to see. I am tempted to stop them from leaving the store so I can ask them about the fifties, sixties, and seventies. Maybe they will give me advance previews into my future, something to prepare me for what lies ahead. But then I realize they have already done that. They are with me every week, living the aches and pains, the physical losses, and the spiritual gains.

They are only church ladies, true. But so am I. We are on the same track, studying the same text, and all of us hope to matriculate to the next level someday. All at once I am overwhelmed by a feeling of safety. These old ladies have my back.

9

LEAVING AHEAD

Many of our customers have a long history with this strangely spiritual place that is the St. Vincent de Paul Thrift Shop. In a way, it belongs to them more than it does to us volunteers. One day I am visiting with a familiar gentlemen who stops in to browse from time to time.

"I see you here a lot," he says to me.

"Usually once a week," I agree, "since 1995."

"Oh, you're just a newcomer," he says with a smile. "This has been my favorite store since the 1960s."

I begin to wonder about other parts of our history. We have a framed document on the wall that tells us that we were "aggregated" in 1926. A story has been passed down of our mission during the Great Depression. The legend is that when all the St. Vincent de Paul money for the poor was lost with the sudden bank closures, the feisty parish priest marched into the bank president's office and laid him out for not warning us ahead of time.

Most poignant for me is a sepia photo of a lovely lady in a 1940s hairstyle and shoulder-padded dress. It hangs above the sorting room door. When I was a new volunteer, Bernie B. told me that the photo must be saved because the lady was the one who donated the property where our store stands.

"What is her name?" I asked, studying the friendly face in the picture.

"No one here remembers anymore," Bernie said. "But it's important not to forget her gift, so we keep the picture hanging there, and from time to time we include her in our prayers."

I carefully dust the photo of our benefactor. We have lost her name, but her smile shines over us every day. The part of her that remains in this world is not her name, not her accomplishments, not her words. What remains is her gift—the St. Vincent de Paul Thrift Store that has become a part of the neighborhood.

It's as if she has *become* her gift. Which is not a bad thing to become.

My next day at St. Vincent de Paul starts out with a man who needs a suit. After trying on every jacket on the rack and finding none to fit, he approaches the cash register and asks me if we have any more in the back room.

"It's not likely, but I could look. What size do you need?"

"A thirty-eight, and I need it today."

That makes me pause. It is Friday morning. Why would he need a suit in a hurry? I ask him.

"It's for my nephew's funeral."

"I'm sorry for your loss," I tell him, but he doesn't reply. We walk to the back room together, and there, hanging by itself, is a suit that has just been donated, wrapped up in a dry cleaner's bag. I pull off the plastic, and he tries the coat on. Perfect. We measure the slacks—exactly his size.

It is so glaringly obvious that this suit was intended for this man that, of course, I wrap it back up and give it to him, compliments of the St. Vincent de Paul Society.

The next week, I am talking with Janice, one of our African-American volunteers, about the coincidence of the suit. She says, "I went to that funeral too. It was for my friend; he left us awfully early. Both his parents left ahead of time too."

I am a little confused. "His parents left in the middle of the funeral?"

She raises her eyebrows at me. "No, no, I told you; they went on ahead. His parents died when he was just a youngster. All his family has gone on ahead of him. First his parents and aunts and uncles, and next his brothers and sisters, and finally him—they all kept leaving him behind, and now he's the last to go. He kept saying he didn't know why God wanted everyone to leave so soon."

Understanding dawns, finally, and I try to explain myself. "In my family, when someone dies, we say we lost them. But I like the way you say it better. . . . *They go on ahead.* That's a hopeful way of seeing it."

Janice looks at me sideways. "We don't *lose* people. Leastways, nobody gets lost that we know of."

There is a revealing element of our faith in the words we choose to speak. Do I believe that someone who dies is lost? No, not most of them anyway. Do I believe they have gone on ahead of me? Yes, I do. Next time someone tells me they are going to a funeral, instead of saying, "I'm sorry for your loss," I'll try to remember to say, "I'm sorry they left you so soon."

In many ways my fellow volunteers are going on ahead. They have been doing this work decades longer than I have, leading the way and sometimes pulling me through the narrower passages. In their shining but tired faces and their strong but stooped shoulders, I am beginning to see my own path more clearly.

My husband's uncle is a retired Lutheran minister who regularly visits people in nursing homes as a volunteer. When I ask about the work he is doing, he tells me, "Well, Jane, I've learned that people don't become sweet little old ladies and sweet little old men just by growing old. If a person doesn't work at being agreeable, then it's not going to happen. I'd say there is as much sweetness and as much cussedness in nursing homes as anywhere else."

It's clear to me that being a volunteer isn't necessarily going to raise my holiness credentials either. As with anything else I've done in my life, it's more about the quality than the quantity. I earnestly want to figure this out while I'm living the best part of my youth. I'm afraid that the coming aches and pains may make me fail miserably at the sweet part of old age. And after I go on ahead, even if everyone forgets my name and what I've accomplished, if the people who have my picture some day in the future don't recognize my face, I want, somehow, to have become a gift.

All my fellow volunteers are getting older, but Dorothy is past ninety, and that mile marker worries me. She has fallen a few times now. Her wrist didn't heal well after she broke it, and it can bother her when she runs the cash register for a couple of hours. There is so much I can learn from her, but I sense that time is running out. What's more, work at the store is increasing and drawing my attention away from her. We work on different days now, and I share a shift with her only once a month or so. I'm not sure if this distance is God's idea or mine. The chances are nearly 100 percent that Dorothy will be leaving ahead of me. It is not something I want to think about.

10

IT'S NOT ABOUT THE REFRIGERATORS

Take care not to spoil God's work by trying to hurry them too much. Take good time and know how to wait. Too often we spoil good works by going too fast, because we are acting according to our own inclinations which makes us think what we want to do is practical and timely. What God wishes done is accomplished almost by itself, without our thinking about it.
—St. Vincent de Paul

My husband informs me that he is going out in the truck on Saturday morning to pick up some refrigerators.

"*Some* refrigerators?" I question. "Do you mean more than one?"

"Yes, there are an even dozen, and they're all in working condition. It's a great donation."

I chew my lip at this point, but Dean doesn't seem to notice. He explains that he has been talking to the leadership of the local papermakers union. Kalamazoo was once known as a "mill town" because of the combination of abundant forests in Michigan, the availability of clean water to make paper, and cheap local labor. Now one of the last remaining paper mills is closing its doors in order to "benefit the shareholders" by moving the work to a far-off land with still-abundant forests, unsullied water, and cheap local labor. Although the company will be shutting down the facility by simply walking away from the huge building filled with all the machines and equipment, the union members have decided to donate the refrigerators from the break rooms, which they had outfitted themselves.

Dean says, "It's generous of these guys to think about others at a time when they are losing their jobs."

I see his point, but at this moment, I'm thinking more about my husband's back. To ease my worries, Dean reassures me that he will call his list of high school volunteers, and since it is already Friday evening, he picks up the phone and starts punching numbers. For some reason he is surprised when most of the students have other plans. At last Jeremy, a rather new volunteer but a brawny one, agrees to sign on. Dean is confident that if they work fast and if he can persuade a couple of the union guys to help load the truck, the job might take only half a day.

"Jeremy lives within sight of the paper mill," Dean tells me as he counts the bungee cords in the back of the truck. "But he says he's never been inside it before. He sounded interested in seeing the place."

"He's still only one high school kid," I point out. "Don't you think you'll need some more help?"

Dean smiles and pecks me on the cheek. "Oh, probably. That's why I'm going to pick up the two-wheeled dolly at St. Vinnie's on the way."

The next morning Dean drives across town, collects the dolly, then heads over to pick up Jeremy. I've often observed that my husband is as easy to talk to as the inside of a refrigerator. Open him up and a light goes on, revealing nonthreatening comfort on multiple levels. Everything is fair game except the raw meat, and if you don't like vegetables, that drawer on the bottom won't open by itself if you just leave it alone.

On these Saturday morning trips with the high school students, the truck windows are rolled down, and the radio is turned up. This is already happening when Dean stops at Jeremy's house in a pocket neighborhood tucked behind a quick-chicken stand and two nail salons. Jeremy, dressed in jeans and a hooded sweatshirt, is waiting when Dean pulls into the driveway. He hops up into the cab, straps on the seat belt, and rests an elbow out the window, and they are on their way.

Turning in the direction of the looming mill, whose four smokestacks punctuate the sky like unnecessary exclamation points, Dean starts the conversation with, "It's good of your dad to share you on a Saturday. St. Vinnie's really needs the help this morning."

Jeremy's lips tighten. He looks straight out the windshield and says, "My dad's in prison. He's been there since I was two years old."

Dean offers the kind of awkward apology that one says at such moments and keeps driving. The easy conversationalist is momentarily derailed. The music helps, and the mill is a short drive across the rail spurs, so they get there without needing to say more. As they pull up to the padlocked chain-link gate, Jeremy leans forward in the cab to peer at the huge, hundred-year-old brick walls stretching 250 feet in three directions.

"*Man,*" he says. "It's even bigger up close."

"Hundreds of guys used to work here at its peak," Dean tells him.

There is a guardhouse next to the gates, but no one is in it. After a few minutes, Dean taps the truck's horn a couple of times and begins to wonder if his information is faulty. Another few minutes go by before five men dressed in nondescript work clothes emerge from a jumble of smaller buildings attached like lean-tos to the main factory.

Dean raises a hand to the men, but they do not bother themselves with such pleasantries.

Two of the guys unlock the gate and slide it out of the way before motioning the truck through. Dean pulls forward, and directed by their hand signals, he swings around in order to back up to a set of double-hung doors in one of the low buildings. He turns off the ignition, jumps out, and walks over to shake hands with the men. They are scowling at our pickup truck. The nearest one asks, did we get the message that there are *twelve* refrigerators to move?

Dean nods cheerfully and assures them that he and Jeremy are prepared to make several trips. The men shake their heads and spit resignedly at the ground.

Jeremy climbs down from the truck, still staring at the shear mass of the building, and hangs back while the men discuss the logistics of moving twelve refrigerators from several locations inside the convoluted factory. After a few minutes, Dean waves his young helper forward and introduces him.

The men nod without smiling and put out their hands to shake his. Jeremy hesitates slightly, caught off guard at being treated in such an adult fashion. But then he recovers, pulls his hands from his pockets, and mimics both their solemn expressions and their firm grips. Dean notices that Jeremy's back straightens half an inch taller as they follow the men into the gloom of the building.

Four refrigerators are standing inside the door. Dean and Jeremy strap the first one onto the dolly and tip it at a traveling angle. The five paper-mill workers stand back and watch. Dean doesn't ask for help getting the appliance onto the truck, and they don't offer any. He and Jeremy manage okay, but it does require several minutes. When they come back inside for the next one, two of the workers shimmy the refrigerator onto the dolly and then follow them outside to help hoist it onto the truck. With the extra hands, the third and fourth appliances get dispatched more efficiently, and Dean and Jeremy drive away with promises to return as soon as possible.

When they get back, the guys are waiting by the gate. Unasked, Dean explains how the St. Vincent de Paul Society helps people and offers gratitude on behalf of the future recipients of their gifts. For the first time, the men show some interest.

It's a long walk to the other refrigerators. For much of the next five minutes they wind their way through a cavernous room with the only light coming from windows three stories above their heads. Their path leads them around hulking steel machinery rising from the dusty concrete floor up to the height of the windows and spreading out in all directions. While Dean and Jeremy gape at the enormous drive gears, shafts, and steel plates, the union guys are chatting about their unplanned retirement.

"The turkeys were right up on the porch this morning stealing the deer feed. My wife was pretty mad about it."

His friends nod. "With the snow that first morning of the season, I thought the hunting would be awesome, but we saw two doe and then nothing for three days. How'd you do?"

"Got a six."

"Something, anyway."

"You see the Packers game on Sunday?"

One of them shakes his head and makes a circle with his arms. "I find the local cable channels on the satellite, but I've only got a hole in the trees like so. If I get a good enough signal I can pick up Canada, but nothing this time."

They turn a corner and Jeremy stumbles from looking too much vertically. "What is that for?" he blurts out, staring at the monster machine in their direct path. It appears to be two stories high with huge pipes coming out of it like crooked candles on a birthday cake. Enormous acid baths sit idle at one side, and room-size rollers come out of the opposite end.

The union guys interrupt their conversation and look around to where he is pointing. "That?" the first one asks. "We call that one Bertha. She's the mother of all paper machines. I worked here eight years before they let me so much as oil her."

They turn to go on, but Jeremy is stuck in a type of rapture. "How does it work?" he asks.

The first guy nudges the second, and for an instant, a corner of his mouth lifts slightly. "Well now, Bertha is the NFL of paper making—she's big-time. You work next to her in the summer, and the temperature is easily over a hundred degrees."

"Isn't that dangerous?" Jeremy asks.

"Not much." Two of the men hold up their hands and show five missing digits between them. "This is the dangerous part," one of them says with a grin.

Then something beautiful happens.

Dean, who has formed a plan for his Saturday that involves the removing of refrigerators from a factory, realizes that refrigerators can wait. The union men become aware for the first time that they are in the presence of an awestruck youth. Jeremy is listening to everything they have to say with parted lips and a brain exploding with fascination.

And it's all about them.

The questions flow from Jeremy so fast that the guys can hardly keep up. They find themselves explaining the last twenty years of their working lives to an audience hungry to hear every word. For the next hour, Dean follows the men and their fan club up into the catwalks and behind the gear shafts. He hears stories of skill, danger, power, and fear.

Up close to the ceiling, the men show them a steel I beam, twisted 180 degrees, sawn off roughly, and embedded in a jumble of backfilled masonry.

"That's from the boiler explosion in '37," one man recalls. "Nearly brought the main building down. There was serious talk they'd have to close the plant rather than rebuild. But the workers pitched in and had production back on line in a much shorter time than anyone thought could happen."

Another worker points to where a main wall was opened up and truck bays put in. He explains to Jeremy, "When new equipment and technology changed the way the work flowed through the plant, one of the line guys suggested to the foreman that if we moved the bays there, it would save thirty minutes per roll to unload the spooler and hoist it onto the trucks. It cost the company a bundle to brace the wall and put the new construction in, but they more than made up the money in a couple years. The front office loved it."

As Dean watches, dejected men revive under the influence of one man-starved youth. All of them become animated and restored as Jeremy asks his questions and they tell their stories.

Late in the afternoon, the men move the last of the refrigerators onto the truck, but that hardly bears mentioning. Their gift is not the refrigerators, and Jeremy's gift is not the *lifting* of the refrigerators. It's not about the refrigerators at all.

11

OUR LADY OF PEACE

Dear Children, . . .
You wish to receive graces, but you do not pray.
I am not able to help you if you do not decide to begin. . . .
I want to teach you to pray.
——OUR LADY OF MEDJUGORJE, JUNE 12, 1986

It is the feast of Our Lady of Ransom, and I am flying over northern Italy on my way to Bosnia. This is an old-calendar feast that commemorates the apparition of Mary to St. Peter Nolasco in 1218. She appeared to this French nobleman and asked him to travel to Spain, where he was instructed to establish a religious order of men whose purpose would be to ransom slaves with either prayer or money or, if those failed, by exchanging themselves. This simple idea had mixed results, freeing 11,615 captives and producing 400 martyrs. St. Peter was one of the martyrs on Christmas Day, 1256.

My reflections on this story, as I stare out the tiny plane window, go something like this: Mary is known to make difficult requests. Since I am traveling to a place where she is reportedly speaking, I am concerned about this habit of hers.

The flight attendant is serving lunch, so I decide to give my copy of *The Lives of the Saints* a rest for now. The landscape below me is rugged, low mountains, and the food on the tray in front of me looks similar. I poke my plastic fork into the lumpy sauce, but there isn't anything that looks like cabbage to me. I taste it and decide it is some form of nonspecific meat, but the breading is tasty.

We are traveling as a group of thirty-one people, two-thirds of us female, ranging from twelve years old to eighty-three. Martha has some connection to nearly all of us—even the priest, Fr. Daryl, is from her hometown. He is a tall young man who laughs readily and has visited Medjugorje a number of times before this.

The rest of us are also happy to be on this adventure but not nearly as relaxed about it as Fr. Daryl. I am not used to plane travel and am definitely not accustomed to being part of a large tour group. It feels unnatural to be traveling without my family, something I have never done before. Even more psychologically uncomfortable are these near-strangers traveling with me who are turning out to be spiritually intimidating.

They pray *all the time*.

In Chicago, at O'Hare Airport, before we even left the ground, between check-in and takeoff, we went looking for a chapel in order to celebrate Mass together. I didn't even know there was such a thing as an airport chapel. The one we found was nondenominational, had lovely stained glass, and trembled every time a plane passed overhead, which lent fervor to my petitions.

Between Chicago and Frankfurt, Germany, I must have recited five rosaries with my seatmate, but on this last leg to Split, Croatia, she has dozed off, and I am finally able to pull out my Croatian language notes and begin cramming. Along with Mary Vrbancic's instructions, I have with me a list of handy phrases from Dean's Aunt Ann, whose parents also were from Croatia. I memorize the words for *left, right, I am tired,* and *I have an American passport.* At the bottom of the page Aunt Ann has written a Croatian saying:

Ne uči papa moliti, ne uči žena kuvati.

Which she translates loosely as "Don't teach a pope to pray; don't teach a woman to cook."

I puzzle over this for quite awhile. *What obscure life lesson is hiding here? What kind of truth is this?*

The plane lands at the airport in Split, Croatia. We wait in our seats until they roll an aluminum staircase across the tarmac and affix it to the side of the aircraft. There are no other planes in sight, only one small building, and I am relieved to note there aren't any machine-gun-toting guards like the ones we saw in the Frankfurt airport.

At least . . . *I think* that's a good sign.

At this point I have been traveling twenty-two hours and have been unable to sleep. The software in my brain is moving slowly and even stalling completely at times. Because of this, it is essential that the woman tour guide help us locate our bags, shepherd us through customs, and load us onto a bus. She is cheerful, organized, and extremely punctual. She also points a lot, which helps.

I was hoping I would be able to sleep on this part of the trip, but it is bright daylight, and everyone else in the group is chatty and full of excitement. They must have slept on the plane.

After we leave the city of Split, we drive along the most beautiful coastal highway I have ever seen. The water of the Adriatic is a changeable aqua color and dotted with islands, which we view from a twisty highway that hugs the craggy hills. We say the rosary as a group, but I keep losing my place on the beads because I am continually dropping them in order to snap pictures out the window of the bus. This will happen multiple times all week long; me dropping Hail Marys like a knitter dropping stitches. I know I am on a pilgrimage, and prayer is a large part of the plan, but I have never been a competent multitasker; hence, a large portion of the grace I should be receiving gets lost in the landscape. At home in my everyday existence, I might have a fighting chance of concentrating on all these prayers, but the Dalmatian coast and farther along the road, war-torn Bosnia, are both highly distracting in their own way. I have never seen such startlingly blue water, nor have I ever seen so many bullet marks in the sides of buildings.

Three hours later we arrive in the little parish of Medjugorje, divide up into the various hostels, and receive instructions on where to meet for supper. Weariness makes it hard to keep my eyes from crossing. I go up to my room and learn there is hot water only in the morning, but the room is clean, modern, and comfortable, so I brush my teeth and go back downstairs to meet the rest of the group for the evening meal.

Like every pilgrim in this backwater village, I am housed in the extra rooms of a local family's home. After the word got out that Mary was appearing here, and the deluge of pilgrims began to arrive, it quickly became apparent that there were no Best Western hotels nearby. The villagers, who were mostly subsistence farmers, began renting out rooms. It wasn't long before they put away their hoes and picked up carpenter's squares instead, in order to add on more rooms. Within a few short years, Mary's appearances changed the local economy from agriculture to inn keeping. The members of our host family have learned to speak smatterings of half a dozen languages, and this includes enough English to confuse us. When we speak to them, no matter what we say, they nod and hand us a map of the village and a schedule of Masses at St. James Church.

After we are all gathered, we are shown into the dining room and seated on benches at several long tables. When they begin bringing the food, I use all the Croatian Mary Vrbancic has taught me. Our hosts stare at me in wonder. They make me repeat my comments for everyone in the family and discuss it with much hand waving and giggling among themselves. I get the idea they have never before heard phrasing quite like mine. I begin to suspect that my fellow Vincentian, Mary, speaks Croatian with a full range of the vernacular, something like the way she speaks English. The other pilgrims at the table are impressed in different ways.

As we wait for the food to be served, the woman next to me discreetly pulls a small jar of peanut butter out of her purse and holds it in her lap. When she sees me watching, she whispers, "This is my second trip, so I've learned how to survive the meals. You're welcome to some if you like."

I thank her but shake my head in refusal. I can't imagine eating peanut butter for a week. *Surely, the food has to be better than that?*

For our supper, our hosts serve us each an entire fish, with the head and tail still intact, fried with a crusty-spicy coating, and resting artfully on a plateful of boiled cabbage. It is absolutely delicious. I eat my neighbor's, too. I think I'm going to like Medjugorje just fine.

12

ATTEMPTING TO BELIEVE

We have many wonderful volunteers at the St. Vinnie's shop in Kalamazoo, and an equal number of ordinary ones, like me. By an "ordinary" volunteer, I mean someone who handles the work of helping the poor with a spotty grace.

One of my fellow Vincentians says to me one day, "Jane, do you have a minute to talk? Something's been bothering me here, and I just need to ask how you deal with it."

I put down what I am doing and give him my full attention. There is nothing more flattering than to be asked for advice. We sit down in a couple of chairs, and he says, "I'm really struggling with some of our clients who come in here. They just don't seem to be on a road that's *moral*." He describes a woman he interviewed the week before who had five children, all with different last names. She was living off government assistance and was unable to pay her utility bill, which is why she came to us for help.

My fellow volunteer and his wife raised five children also, putting them all through college. Now retired, he feels blessed and wants to give back for all he has received. But this woman's situation seemingly goes against everything he values—nuclear family, personal responsibility, self-sufficiency. He promised her some financial assistance but he wasn't feeling the joy.

"How do we even know if these people are telling us the truth?" he grumbles. "Sure, we call the utility companies or the landlords to check the specifics on the bill, and then we find out what the Department of Human Services workers know, but even then we may not be getting the straight version of things."

I look at him sympathetically and decide to tell him a couple of stories, which is something of a habit with me.

The Family with Six Last Names

I am interviewing a young mother who needs help with one of her bills. While filling in the paperwork, I ask for names of the other members of the household. She gives me her fiancé's name, then the full names of all four children. Everyone in this family has a different last name. I make no comment, and we move on down the form to the section about income. I ask her if she receives child-support payments for any of the children.

She answers, "I told you their dad works at the Amoco station."

I stop writing. "Do you mean your fiancé is the father of all four kids?"

She nods happily. "We've been together for fifteen years, ever since high school."

"But—" It feels strange to ask, but I do it anyway. "Why do all the children have different last names?"

"Oh, I see why you're confused," she says. "See, when our oldest was born, my aunt was real sick and looking like she was ready to pass, so we gave him her last name on account of she didn't have any children of her own."

"You can do that?"

The young mother flaps a hand at me. "Sure you can. The hospital people don't mind what you call the baby as long as the mother is listed properly. Our son has my fiancé's father's name, then the second daughter has my mother's name, and we blessed my other aunt by calling the baby with her name."

I must look a bit dumbfounded, because that's how I feel.

She smiles at me and says, "Those last names don't matter much anyway because they are just slave-master names. The first names of our children came straight from our hearts; my fiancé and I wrote them together."

She is obviously proud of her family, and I can't help but be proud for her. "Thank you for explaining this to me. I expect you aren't the only family who gives different last names to their children?"

She shrugs good humouredly, "It doesn't make a lot of sense to name everybody the same if you don't have to."

When I finish, my fellow Vincentian looks aghast. "You're kidding me," he says bluntly.

"God's truth," I tell him. "Are you ready for the next story?"

The Woman's Tears

The woman and her husband are sitting across from each other in our small office. They are nicely dressed in warm winter coats and boots. She wears makeup and has her hair coiffed, and her fingernails look as if they cost more than my shoes. She does all the talking, and that seems to be okay with her husband, and it's also okay by me.

"I'd do anything for my loved ones," she tells me. "These boots I'm wearing are three years old because I can't bear to let my elderly mother go without. If it hadn't been that we needed to move so suddenly, I'd never be here asking for help. This is not something that we're used to, is it, James?" She glances at her husband, but he just gazes back at her with a resigned look on his face. "We always take care of ourselves, and it's nearly killing us to be here."

I ask if they have applied for help at the Department of Human Services, and instantly her face clouds over.

"The people told us we had one of the best workers in the place, but what a lie that was. I have never been so disrespected in my entire life. You wouldn't believe the things that man accused us of doing in our old town. We had to leave home because it was not a safe place for my mother, and that is the only reason we left. Do you think I would tear her away from her church, put all my furniture in storage, and put an eighty-year-old sick woman on a bus with only a small bag of clothing if the situation wasn't desperate? No loving daughter would do that, I tell you. That man at DHS was the rudest, meanest person I have ever met in my life. When I demanded the respect that any American citizen deserves, he called in the security guards, and they escorted us out of the building. They didn't do it without some trouble, I'm telling you, but what good did it do? Here we are with. . . ."

People need to be believed.

It is not possible to have a real relationship with another person if credulity is strained. If I start questioning this lady about her story of pure victimhood, then she will know I don't necessarily believe every word she is saying, and she will, naturally, react badly to my disbelief. There is not going to be any love going back and forth in this room if there is no belief on my part. As a stranger to her, she has no reason to trust me. Therefore, if there is going to be love, it is I who must make the attempt to find *something* in her that I can accept.

So, I am listening intently to the woman's story, searching hard for anything that rings true. She notices my earnestness and warms to me, but to my dismay, the drama continues to inflate. Clearly in the groove of her narrative now, she tells me about the crooked landlord at her former apartment who refused to return the security deposit, the unreasonable rules at the homeless shelter that forced them onto the street, and the lawsuit she will be bringing against the State of Michigan. Slumped in his chair, her husband watches silently, his chin resting in the palm of his hand.

This believing effort is straining me to the point where my sense of the ridiculous is about to burst forth. *Not a good idea*, I tell myself.

Instead, I begin looking over her paperwork, trying to find some unequivocal reason to deny her monetary help, anything that puts her outside our criteria. She keeps talking, and I turn up nothing in the paperwork. Since she is from a different town and we have no record of ever having helped her before, it is up to me to decide whether St. Vincent de Paul money will be made available to her for the security deposit she needs for an apartment. In the end, I figure if our rules will allow me to give this woman a promise of some money, I may as well do it.

It might save me some trouble. We do not have security guards at the St. Vincent de Paul Thrift Store.

I quickly fill out a promissory note and hand it to her saying, "This is a promise for $150. If you find an apartment to rent and can come up with the rest of what you need, you'll have to get at least half of it from other churches or agencies for this to be valid. When you get the rest, you need to bring the paperwork back here and we will send the money in the mail directly to the landlord. Do you have questions on any of this?"

She doesn't answer. She is looking at the note in her hand. I ask again if she understands, and she looks up at me and says, "Yes . . . yes. This is very nice." And then tears come pouring from her eyes, across her cheeks, and down both sides of her nose.

I stare at her in astonishment, and so does her husband. After a moment he fumbles in his pocket and hands her a tissue. She is pushing at the tears, not with her fingers—she needs the palms of her hands in order to stem the flow. "I'm sorry," she says, clearly as befuddled by the tears as we are. "This is good of you. We are grateful. I don't know why . . . I'm going to need another tissue. . . . Goodness, I don't know what's come over me." The tears run on, not one at a time but in rivulets. She is not sobbing. Her voice is a little shaky but not tremulous. These tears have caught her off guard as much as they have us.

"Are you all right?" I ask.

She stands up, flustered, still pushing back at the flood coming down her face. "Yes, yes, we need to go now. We'll be back when we get the rest of the money. Thank you again." Her husband stands also, shaking his head at her, baffled by what he is seeing.

He takes her purse so she can continue to mop up her eyes, and they leave the store.

I am left sitting in the office stunned, slowly putting together what just happened.

My fellow Vincentian is looking very seriously at me as I finish the story. "She was lying," he says.

I shrug. "There's no way to know that for sure, and so I gave her the money anyway and then . . . did I answer your question?"

He looks away, thinking. After a pause, he says, "Yes . . . yes, you did."

I smile at him, and he musters a pained grin. I say, "So don't get the idea I understand everybody who comes in here for help or everything that happens here. I don't. All I know for sure is if I try to act out of love for the person, if I attempt to listen and have sympathy for their situation, then it usually works out for the best. But there are plenty of times where I'm frustrated and confused. The absolute worst situations for me are when I have to interview a really angry man. I get so rattled by shouting—and even implied threats—that love doesn't have a whisper of a chance. Those interviews always end badly."

My friend looks unperturbed and says, "Oh, guys like that don't bother me—they're only bullies. I just give it right back to them until they either get some sense or go away. Sometimes love is just showing them you won't put up with their garbage."

13

PRAY, PRAY, PRAY!

Pray, Pray, Pray!

—OUR LADY OF MEDJUGORJE, 1981

The first morning I wake up in Medjugorje is a beautiful fall day. I look out the window of my room and straight down. Three stories below me is a vegetable garden. Apparently we are near the outskirts of the village, because beyond these rows of cabbages I can see only vineyards and a few groups of freelancing goats. As I look to the horizon in all directions, we seem to be in a valley surrounded by rocky hills, and on the tallest hill stands an enormous concrete cross. I find this on my map and identify it as Mount Krizevac. Even though I don't know the Croatian words for cross or crucifix, either of them might be a logical translation.

To my right and left the neighbors' homes along the gravel street are either stone or stucco, and they all rise two to four stories, owing to the ubiquitous add-on guest rooms. Some construction workers on the street appear to be putting in curbing in preparation for pavement, but they are doing this with shovels and a single old-fashioned, barrel-type cement mixer that sputters and smokes as it sloshes the sand, water, and lime together. At this rate, the project will keep them employed a good many weeks.

Checking my map again, I identify the top of St. James Church, its twin stucco spires rising against the blue sky about half a mile away in the center of the village. The English-speaking Mass is scheduled for ten, so I dress quickly and go downstairs to breakfast. In order to keep the small fast, I want to finish eating an hour before Mass. The food—oranges, bread, slices of white cheese, and bologna—is on the tables in large platters. Most of our group is already seated and eating, so I slide onto the nearest bench and am pleased to be served *kava sa mlijeko*—coffee with milk. Pointing at the bread, I ask our hostess, "Kako se ovo zove?" *What do you call this?*

She lowers her face down to my level and slowly repeats the question back to me, correcting my pronunciation and nodding encouragement while I try it again. "Da, da," she says. Then she holds up a slice of bread and enunciates, "Kruh. Kruh."

It turns out that the entire table of pilgrims is watching us, and they all repeat back to her in unison, "*Kruhhh.*" Their sudden interest in the language catches both our hostess and me by surprise. She claps her hands in delight, and we all laugh, pleased with ourselves for the rest of the mealtime.

I soon learn that I have become a hero to several of the food-challenged pilgrims. They now have the ability to ask for the bread they need to go with their peanut butter.

After breakfast we gather in front of the house and head toward the church. It is Saturday, not Sunday, but that doesn't matter, because Mass is scheduled nearly every hour every day of the week. One of the first things Our Blessed Mother told the visionaries when she arrived in their town was that everyone needed to go to Mass more often. She spelled this out to mean *every day, if possible*. She told them she hoped to make the village into an example of faith for the entire world, and Mass was where they would begin. This is one of the most convincing elements of the whole apparition story for me. The visionaries were teenagers when all this started . . . and teenagers would not make this part up.

We arrive at the church ten minutes early and discover that the only places remaining are in the shoulder-to-shoulder standing room in the back. We find ourselves scrunched next to a pillar that blocks our view of half the altar, but that's the best we can do. When Mass begins, there are a half dozen priests up front, with an Australian priest presiding. A group of Australian pilgrims proclaim all the readings, too, and even though I know they are speaking English, I catch only about two-thirds of what they say.

The essence of the homily today is that Mary has come to ask the world to pray. She began by teaching the people of Medjugorje to pray, and from there, she hopes to convince the rest of us. And what does she want us to pray about?

Peace.

"Pray for peace," she told the people of the town in 1981. They looked at each other in confusion. There hadn't been a war in their country since 1945; why would she come all the way from heaven to tell them this? War or no war, they complied, and they began to pray for peace even though they already had plenty of peace.

In April 1991, ten years later, after Yugoslavia broke apart, the Bosnian War began.

While we are sitting in St. James Church listening to this sermon, United Nations soldiers sit in their trucks outside, and NATO helicopters thrum overhead on their way to Kosovo.

"And what else does the mother of God want us to pray for?" The Australian priest asks the congregation.

"'*Pray for young people*,' she tells us, 'and *pray for the priests*.'"

I am listening intently on account of her prescience concerning the war. *Pray for young people?* Okay, I'm on it. I am a teacher, and I love young people. There are a lot of reasons to pray for them too. Simultaneous worldwide epidemics of broken families, teen pregnancies, drug and alcohol abuse, and depression all affect young people tremendously. Education is more and more expensive, and jobs are scarce. I pray for them all the time already, so this is not a problem for me.

Pray for priests? Um. . . . Why exactly do priests need more prayers than anyone else? Why not pray for doctors, for instance? Or pray for nuns? Or for the poor? I am feeling a little like the people in Medjugorje must have felt in 1981 when Mary asked them to pray for peace.

Is there something she's not telling us?

When it is time to kneel for the consecration of the bread and wine, I assume that we, who have no pews or kneelers, will remain standing as we would at home. But we are pilgrims on a pilgrimage, and apparently this is not the time to ignore rubrics. All of us who are packed into the rear of the church jostle against each other, lower ourselves to the stone floor, and kneel, not only for the consecration but also clear through the distribution of communion. My knees complain fiercely about the discomfort, but then I spot an elderly lady a few feet away, her arthritic hands gripped around her cane, nonetheless kneeling on the cold stone.

Forget the priests—they are standing up. I will pray for her instead.

Mercifully, because of the tight daily schedule, the entire mass lasts only forty-five minutes, and that includes the litany of the saints.

When it is over, between the claustrophobic crush of the crowd, the confusing sermon, and the pain in my knees, I am glad to get out of that church.

I am a lousy pilgrim.

14

SHIRLEY

So we all have our weak points, our places where we need to be stretched. I run into another one of mine one day when Shirley is working with me at St. Vinnie's.

Shirley raised eight children with her husband on a milkman's salary. Now she is widowed and retired and spends her free time with grandchildren or playing bridge or volunteering at the thrift store.

One day a man comes into St. Vincent and inquires whether he is eligible for free clothing. I am in the back room and don't see the man enter the store, but I become quickly aware that he is present.

The odor is remarkable.

I look through the door onto the sales floor and spot him at the checkout counter speaking with one of our cashiers. One customer near me checks the bottom of his own shoes, and others begin to head for the door. We can't afford to lose customers, but we don't want to embarrass the man either. I breeze out into the store and announce, "The day sure is warming up! Perhaps we can open the door." I make straight for the front of the building, fling open the door, and prop it with a brick.

I return to the checkout and find Shirley conversing with the gentleman. He is in need of some clothes, he tells her, and she finds nothing to disagree with. "That's a good plan," she tells him. "Why don't you come with me, sir, and we'll get you all set up." Breathing through my mouth, I ask Shirley if she needs any help, but she winks at me and waves me off. "Oh, I'll be glad to help this gentleman, Jane. You go ahead and take your break."

I gratefully retreat to the back room, but the stench seems to be soaking into the walls of the building. There is no escaping it. I want to flee further into the warehouse, but Shirley's casual martyrdom has me fascinated. I put a sleeve to my face and proceed to watch the most heroic act of haberdashery in the history of the St. Vincent de Paul Society.

She leads him first to the shirts and helps him pick out two that she convinces him to take into the dressing room and try on straightaway. He argues that they are certain to fit and that modeling them isn't necessary, but she won't hear of it and orders him to show her each shirt in turn so that she can be the judge of whether they fit properly or not. After he appears in the second shirt, she says, "Well, you were right; they both work. Why don't you just leave that one on and put your old shirt in this bag. You really look very well in it, and it's a better fabric for this warm weather." He agrees to that. Next she leads him to the pants, and they go through the whole routine again. By the time he has finished with the slacks, the man is beginning to remark to Shirley about how he has never been waited on as nicely as this in *any* store. She smiles, thanks him modestly, and suggests they look in the underwear and sock drawers. At this point, he surprises everyone by claiming that since he lives on the street and doesn't have any place to keep extra clothing, he doesn't really want any new underwear.

Shirley says, "Oh, but, sir, you will when you go to the Laundromat: one to wear, and one to wash. And it's always a good idea to have extra, especially if you can't get everything dry right away."

He shakes his head and insists that he really has all the underwear and socks he needs, but Shirley won't hear of it. On her own initiative she gathers several pairs and puts them on the checkout counter with the other new clothes. "One to wear and one to wash," she repeats. She double-bags the man's dirty clothes, ties the handles together securely, and puts the extra new clothing in a separate sack. As she hands these to him and acknowledges his thanks with a warm smile, I hear her tell him, "You'd be a very handsome fellow if you only took care of yourself a little better. Now, next time you come in here, I want to see you shaved."

During the years I work with Shirley on Friday afternoons at the St. Vincent de Paul Shop, the priest sex-abuse crisis in the Catholic Church is splashed across our newspaper nearly every week. With more and more revelations and accusations coming out, we, the faithful, slowly begin to take in the enormity of the betrayal by our own hierarchy.

It smudges our spirits like ashes on our foreheads.

It sure hurts when these things happen in the Church. Nobody has the stomach for a situation in which the people you trusted most to teach your children about the love of God have actually been abusing those children. But Catholics are also well-schooled in the dogma of original sin. We know that *all* people do bad things. Every last one of us is a sinner, whether we go to church or not. The only two exemptions from this in the whole history of Christianity are Mary and Jesus, and Jesus doesn't count because he is God. So the fact that some priests turned out to be child-abusers is a nasty business, but it's not a reason to condemn the entire Church. The fact that some bishops let them get away with it for years, however, is the confidence-shaking stuff.

We Catholics also know that there are a lot of very good priests and bishops who are suffering through this situation along with the laity. These men pray over us when we are sick, baptize our babies, assure us of God's forgiveness when we go astray, mourn with us through the death of loved ones, and bless our marriages. Theirs are the hands that consecrate the Holy Mysteries: our daily bread given from heaven.

The relationship between a priest and his flock requires much of both the priest and the flock.

If it doesn't, I guess it's not a real relationship.

There are risks in a real relationship, and when there is wrongdoing, there are always going to be consequences. What these consequences will be is still unfolding, and throughout the Catholic Church there is a collective holding of breath.

While all this is going on, we are holding our noses at the St. Vincent de Paul Society and trying to keep our minds on helping the needy. It isn't easy to shake the news off when it is constantly in front of us. This brings me back to Shirley.

One day at the store, we are eating our lunch together. Shirley is reading the paper and losing her appetite. Eventually she tosses down the pages and says, "This sex-abuse stuff makes me so mad I could spit."

I put down my sandwich and nod in agreement.

She says, "If I was younger I'd leave the church. I'd find a different denomination in a minute if I wasn't eighty already."

I ponder this a moment, thinking about my own age and the implications of her statement. "What difference does it make how old you are?"

Shirley pushes her half-eaten lunch away and sits back in her chair. "If I had known this was going on when I was raising my kids, I would have been out of there in a minute. But now I'm too old to get used to a new church and meet new people. I figure the only way I can show my disgust is to turn up every Sunday and give my money elsewhere."

It is no wonder Mary asked us to pray for priests.

15

RITA AND EVA

It is busy this week at the store. There are shoppers all over the place; the rear doorbell keeps ringing with people who are dropping off donations; and we have a full schedule of appointments for those seeking assistance.

Rita, the first woman in the office, comes with her new friend, Eva. They met each other at the outpatient clinic at the University of Michigan medical center in Ann Arbor. Their friendship warmed in the waiting room; they caught the same Greyhound bus home, and then they helped each other settle into the homeless shelter when they arrived back in Kalamazoo. Eva was in the hospital for tests, and Rita had her right eye removed.

I am chewing on the inside of my cheek while I listen to their story.

They are in our store to ask for assistance with moving out of the shelter. When they are finished telling me their story, I can't help blurting out to Rita, "They removed your eye in an outpatient clinic and *sent you home on a bus*? Doesn't a person need follow-up treatment for that?"

Rita shrugs. "I'm supposed to go to the emergency room at the hospital here if it starts to act up." Then she chuckles a little and says, "I went yesterday, but it was a false alarm. See, I was sitting on the city bus, minding my own business, and there was a bunch of kids fooling around, changing seats, tossing things back and forth like kids do. All of a sudden, I felt something in my lap, so I looked down and there's this little white ball. I pick it up and I'm thinking; *Where did that come from? Did those kids toss it at me?* I looked at it a little closer and then I said, 'Uh-oh.' I put my hand to my face and sure enough, it was something that had come out of my eye socket the doctors must have put in there. I tucked it into my pocket, jumped off the bus at the next stop, and got myself over to the emergency room quick as I could."

When she showed it to the emergency room physicians, they weren't sure what it was either, so they called in a staff ophthalmologist, who explained it was a spacer that was temporarily keeping the shape of her eye socket until the mythical day when she could afford a cosmetic false eye. The doctor showed Rita how to pop the plastic ball back in and helped her practice a few times.

Rita is telling me all this with frequent, self-deprecating laughter. I look at Eva, who is looking at her fingernails. I do the same.

They have found neighboring apartments in what was formerly a residence motel, and have come to St. Vincent de Paul to see if we can give them assistance with furniture and household items. Neither of them was able to hold on to any large possessions while they were ill and living at the Gospel Mission between hospital stays, so they are starting over again, building their lives from scratch. They need everything from beds to teaspoons, so I take down their information and promise to stop by their new homes the following Saturday.

"How are you going to pay the rent?" I ask Rita. "Do you have a job?"

She shakes her head. "I'm a Certified Nursing Assistant. I used to work in a nursing home until this problem with my eye started. I haven't been able to work since I got sick, which is why I've been living at the Mission. But this new landlord says he'll take the Section 8 money and let my part rest until I can apply for disability. I've got bone spurs in my spine that give me something called sciatica all the way down in my leg—can you believe that? That's why I use this cane. I also got diabetes on top of the glaucoma that took my eye, so I'm praying it won't be too long before they approve me for being disabled."

"Minimum of two years," Eva says to her. "Don't nobody get it faster than that no matter how sick you are. And you best get a lawyer or you won't get nothing at all."

Rita folds her arms. "And how is a person supposed to pay for a lawyer?" But we all know Eva is speaking the truth.

I watch these two ladies leave the office on each other's arms and start to mentally inventory the furniture in my basement and the linens in my closet.

The next client is a man named Otis. He is in his thirties with a toddler in his arms and a bespectacled fifth grader sitting quietly by his side. The man hands me an eviction notice for a rented house that is only one block away from our store. He truly is our neighbor. I ask if he has been in the store before. He has not. He explains that his girlfriend came to us for help a few weeks ago, but they haven't been able to find all the money they need yet to pay the back rent. I look over the paperwork and agree to extend our promise of money for another few weeks to allow them more time.

Otis is grateful, but it strikes me that his spirits are very low, so I spend some time complimenting him on the behavior of the children and his manner with them. Regretfully, this has the opposite effect from what I intended. He stares at the wall and his lips tighten. He thanks me again and explains about all the bills and how bad it feels not to be able to take care of the children.

There have been just too many sad stories for me today. I stand up and walk across the office to the filing cabinet, unlock it, and take out a small envelope we keep inside. Whenever customers tell us "keep the change," or someone hands us some extra cash, we tuck it into this envelope and redistribute it in the same way—on the spur of the moment, wherever it feels right. Luckily, there is a twenty in the envelope today, so I pull it out and hand it to this depressed man, saying, "Here, Otis, take the kids to McDonald's. You all deserve a small treat."

He bites his lip and turns away, but he takes the money. He stands up, thanks me again, and takes the baby in his arms. Despite my efforts, I can tell he feels worse than when he came in, but I also hope he will get over it when he is eating that hamburger.

At least *I* feel a little better, anyway.

16

CHRISTIANS OUT OF CONTEXT

It's Saturday morning, and Dean is dressed in his favorite weekend garb: red plaid flannel shirt and blue jeans. He skipped shaving and breakfast because he is in a hurry to get going on his weekend mission for the St. Vincent de Paul Society. He thoroughly enjoys running around the county in his pickup truck with the high school and college students, hauling donated furniture. It is a welcome contrast to his stressful career as a small business owner in the unstable life-sciences industry.

This morning they go way outside the city to a prestigious address on the shores of Gull Lake. Many of the homes lining this popular inland lake are mansion-like cottages for wealthy people from all over the Midwest. In summer the waters are clear green-blue, the skiing and sailing are optimal, and the people who live there are generous to charities like ours.

Dean and his two assistants are going after a couch. We are experiencing an early winter snow, but nothing they can't handle. An accumulation of eight inches is already on the ground, with more expected, so Dean throws a half dozen bags of sand and a plastic tarp in the back of the truck, and they head out.

When they arrive at the house, half an hour later, Dean backs into the driveway to make the distance from the door to the truck as short as possible in the slippery footing. It is a walk-out ranch-style home, with most of the windows facing the frozen lake. A three-car garage dominates the street side. Our three volunteers follow the walkway around the garage to the front door and press the bell. A gentleman promptly opens the door, but after Dean introduces himself and his crew, the man hesitates slightly. He looks at their snow-covered boots, their blue jeans, and Dean's stubbly jaw and makes an executive decision.

"The couch is on the lake side of the house," he tells them. "Why don't you walk around to that side and take it out the sliding doors off the patio. I'll meet you there." The door closes, and Dean looks in the direction the man has indicated. It is a steep incline through foot-deep snowdrifts. He realizes that the gentleman has mistaken the three of them for ordinary working stiffs. Apparently he prefers not to have scruffy-looking types walk through his home today.

This amuses Dean.

He hasn't been treated like this in a long time, not since he was a teenager himself. He turns to his helpers. The two young men have looks of disbelief on their faces, which change to resignation when he grins at them and says, "Okay, guys. Let's hope this couch isn't too heavy."

They trudge through the snow, slipping and sliding down the hill and around the end of the house, until they tramp onto the patio. When they reach the sliding door, Dean instructs his crew to remove their boots, as he always does, and they wait patiently in the cold until the gentleman unlocks the door. They pad in their stocking feet across the carpet and pick up the couch.

It's a sleeper sofa.

The students send exasperated looks Dean's way, but he just winks back at them. He can see by now that this adventure might turn out to be the mother of all teaching moments. They move the weighty donation out onto the patio, set it down, and tie on their boots again.

The trip back up the slope takes some time.

When they finally get the thing loaded onto the pickup truck and covered with the tarp, Dean returns to the front door and hands the man a receipt. They are both cordial and grateful, but one of them is covered in snow and sweat and has learned an invaluable lesson about what it's like to be a common laborer.

When Dean returns home, he is tired and wet, but even after hearing the story of the couch, I have no pity. "There are these two women I met at St. Vinnie's who need some furniture. They don't have beds or tables or anything for their apartments. A sleeper sofa would be perfect. Let's take it to them."

I have a very good husband.

I gather up blankets and sheets from my stash of extra in our linen closet and put together a couple of sacks of groceries. My mom, Dottie, who lives with us, sees what we are doing and offers to contribute some food too. Then all three of us hop into the truck and go back to the thrift store, which is already closed for the day. We load the sofa back onto the truck and tuck a couple of chairs and tables along the sides.

I can tell from the looks on their faces that Rita and Eva are not expecting us at all. They are amazed and excited to see all the things we have brought, and Dean is relieved that they live in ground-floor apartments. The apartments are old and drafty, but they seem to be clean. Rita has a lamp, and Eva a television. That's the sum of all their furnishings. After the St. Vincent de Paul Society is finished unloading, they each get a table and a chair, a few kitchen items, a set of sheets, and two blankets, and they have a sleeper sofa to share for the time being.

We get a lot of hugs.

As we drive away, the windshield wipers push the snow across the glass.

The next week, Dean is one of the presenters at a forum for venture capital investors. He is cleanly shaven and dressed in his workday pressed shirt, conservative tie, and suit jacket. The PowerPoint presentation goes well, and afterward he answers questions about trends in the life-sciences industry and economic forecasts.

When he leaves the podium and begins networking with the forum participants, he is introduced to a man who looks very familiar. Dean smiles as they exchange business cards.

Shaking hands, the man closes one eye and scrutinizes my husband closely, "Excuse me," he says, "but . . . aren't you the guy who took away my old couch on Saturday?"

17

CLIMBING MOUNT KRIZEVAC

My friend Tom has already been to Medjugorje. On his trip the war was closer, and the United Nations had set up a base in the town because it was one of the few villages free of active fighting. Tom is one of those people who sometimes ignore warnings in embassy guidelines. This character trait led him to explore the surrounding countryside more than would ordinarily be recommended in a war-ravaged land.

During a particularly interesting excursion, he somehow caught a ride in a Blazer with a couple of United Nations Stabilization Force soldiers from Canada and Belgium. They wedged him behind the front seats with strict orders not to kick the bag at his feet because it was full of ammunition.

"What do you do at home?" the Belgian asked him when they were under way.

"I'm a high school teacher."

The Canadian turned around to look at Tom more closely. "A teacher, eh? Make sure when you get back to the States that you tell your students how wars get started."

Tom leaned forward and said, "Today I was in a village where there wasn't a place you could put your hand on a wall without touching a bullet hole."

The soldiers nodded grimly and the Belgian said, "Tell your students that this could happen in America. When people turn evil, war can happen anywhere, and it happens quick." They pulled up at Tom's destination to let him out and gave him one final bit of advice: "Don't step on the sand; stay on the rocks."

When Tom is telling me this story, he also tells me about a former soldier who survived when his entire platoon was killed in an all-night bombing raid. During the firefight, this man pledged to the Blessed Virgin of Medjugorje that if his life was spared, he would climb Mount Krizevac on his knees.

Surviving a war is one thing; climbing a mountain like this one on your knees ranks somewhat lower, but not a ton lower. Mount Krizevac is 452 meters of sharp rocks, slippery red clay, and bramble bushes. Granted, this is not a large mountain by any stretch of the imagination, but spiritual pilgrims are not mountain climbers either. The average hiker on this trail is more likely to be wearing a fanny pack and tennis shoes than oxygen tanks and crampons.

There is a worn path that the pilgrims scramble up. Their thousands of rubber-soled shoes have not succeeded in softening the edges of the jagged stone, nor have they made the squishy clay less treacherous, but the brambles usually won't grab hold of their clothes as long as they keep their balance and don't fall off the path.

The first full day in Medjugorje, our group is following Fr. Daryl up Mount Krizevac as he leads us in the Stations of the Cross along the way. This is a devotional meditation on Jesus' horrific struggle through Jerusalem carrying the cross to Golgotha, where he was crucified. Today is overcast and chilly, so the prayer form fits the weather, the taxing physical effort, and my mood. Because of the narrowness of the trail, we are climbing in single file, with many of our older members taking frequent pauses to catch their breath. When I reach a large, illustrated bronze plaque marking the first station, about half of the group is already gathered, leaning or sitting on rough rocks, waiting for the rest of us. After we all arrive, Fr. Daryl begins with an Our Father.

Then he announces, *"The First Station: Jesus Is Condemned to Death."*

To which we all reply, *"We adore you, O Christ, and we bless you, because by your holy cross, you have redeemed the world."*

Father shares a few thoughts with us on betrayal and injustice, which sober my mood even more, and then we resume our climb.

For good reason, this particular devotional form of prayer is an appropriate plan for going up this mountain. There are fourteen of these stations marked by bronze plaques at somewhat level locations, which allow us to catch our breath every fifty feet or so on the switchback trail. It goes like this: climb at a fifteen- to thirty-degree

erratic incline; every few yards allow downward-bound pilgrims to pass in the narrow spots; give a hand to our
less able-bodied companions over the larger rocks; gather
around the plaque, counting everyone as they arrive; then
pray in unison for a couple of minutes, meditating on the
Lord's last walk through the streets of Jerusalem on Good
Friday. This works well for concentrating our minds on
prayer while at the same time setting a reasonable pace for
the older ones among us.

In the beginning there is some chatter among the pilgrims, and several stop to snap photographs. But as we
pass the stations that mark the moments when Jesus is
burdened with the wooden cross, when he falls the first
time, and when he meets his mother, we are less inclined
to look at the view and become more focused on looking
within.

By now, we are all starting to feel aches in our legs,
so when Fr. Daryl announces the place where *Simon the
Cyrene Takes the Cross off Jesus' Shoulder*, we grunt with real
empathy, and when *Veronica Wipes the Lord's Face* with her
veil, we pull our own sleeves across our brows.

Shortly after this, a light rain begins falling, which
quickly makes the trail the consistency of oatmeal studded
with sharp, rocky tines poking up every few inches. This is
not part of the planned prayer scheme, but it is typical of
ordinary life, so we zip our jackets and trudge on. At the
seventh station—*Jesus Falls the Second Time*—one of our
members falls flat on her face. (This is painfully ironic, but
no one likes to mention it.) After we pick her up and exam-
ine her bloody hands and knees, several volunteers offer to

help her back down the mountain. We don't exactly fight over the honor, but the two winners look jubilant as they reverse course, supporting the limping lady as they go.

I grew up and have spent most of my life in Michigan. We do not have many mountains in our state, and those we do have are covered with soft pine needles and wildflowers. Wherever nature gets treacherous, we build boardwalks and post "seasonal road" warning signs. I wonder, while I scramble and slide my way up this wet hill, why the people who installed the brass plaques did not think to drill a few handrails in the rocks while they were at it.

At the eighth station, *Jesus Meets the Women of Jerusalem,* it occurs to me that I am probably supposed to find some spiritual truth in all this mud. I prefer to look for God in orderliness and conviction, but that might be why my search has had mixed results. I am feeling neither order nor conviction in flying across the ocean to Bosnia to pray at the top of this craggy hill. But I am a good student, and good students go where the teacher leads.

"Jesus Falls the Third Time." I watch my footing carefully.

"Jesus Is Stripped of His Garments." I zip my coat higher.

"Jesus Is Nailed to the Cross." I shudder, remembering bullet holes in stucco walls.

"Jesus Dies. . . . His Body Is Taken Down. . . ." and *". . . He Is Laid in the Tomb."*

It is finally over. I am almost to the top of this mountain, and the enormous concrete cross is within sight. I am simultaneously sweaty and cold, and ready to be done with these two hours of morose, trudging prayers.

We turn the last corner, and there is . . . *another station? That's not right.*

I am a cradle Catholic, and I know these things. There are *fourteen* Stations of the Cross. I was tested on this before my Confirmation. I know there are only fourteen.

What good does it do to belong to a religion that is two thousand years old if they are going to change things? For heaven's sake—if I wanted trendiness and cultural relevance, I would not be a Roman Catholic.

Fr. Daryl is standing in front of the bronze plaque, blocking my view, so I maneuver myself around to get a good look at this tomfoolery. It is a picture of Jesus elevating above his tomb.

The Fifteenth Station: Jesus Rises from the Dead.

I sit down on the nearest boulder, disgruntled. *How is a person supposed to instantly change from cold, wet, spiritual gloom to ecstatic joy? Give me three days, and perhaps I could make the psychological switch, but no way is it going to happen in a few yards on a muddy trail.*

The rest of our group gradually gathers, and we say the prescribed prayers. Fr. Daryl shares some uplifting thoughts about heavenly places that totally pass me by. I'm soaking wet, my fingers are frozen, my soul is burdened, and I am in no mood.

18

QUESTIONING CONVICTIONS

The St. Vincent de Paul Thrift Shop is across the street from a family homeless shelter. This is an excellent location for us. One of our unbreakable rules is that we must meet the people we help face-to-face, because that is where we will meet Jesus. St. Vincent once said, "We do our work to find God in it, rather than just to get it done."

One day a father and his six small children troop single file into the thrift store. The tops of the little ones' heads are staggered at four inch intervals of height, like stair steps. At first, we clerks exchange glances, doubting whether one lone man is sufficient to keep twelve little hands off the breakables, but we needn't have worried. The children follow along behind him to the back of the store and wait patiently while he begins searching the clothing for their sizes.

Watching this scene, an elderly gentleman shopper hands our cashier a ten and tells her, "Whatever that father buys, use this to pay for it." Then he leaves.

A few minutes later, when the family comes up to the cash register and Joan totals up the sale, she tells the father his purchase is not only covered but there is $1.50 left over. Dad looks at us in surprise and then at his children and says, "Come on, kids, let's get another shirt for each of you." They are all for that, and the orderly line returns to the clothing racks.

This is the point in the story where one begins to believe seriously in angels.

A woman customer, overhearing, whispers to our cashier that she would like to cover whatever *else* the father decides to purchase.

When the family returns to the checkout and finds that their additional clothing is also free, the father looks momentarily incredulous. But then a huge smile breaks over his face. "Kids," he says to them, "we're going for ice cream!"

When I tell people this story, many of them are as delighted with it as I am, but curiously, some people don't like it at all. One opinion out there says: *That father should have saved his money. Spending it on something as frivolous as ice cream is a waste of the gift he was given.*

Hmm. Okay, that's logical.

But at the time it happened, that's not how I saw it at all.

I saw an older gentleman who was touched by God to purchase the clothing this family needed. I saw a father who, at first, took this gift as a sign that God wanted him to buy more clothing for his children. But on the occasion of the second gift, I saw a father who was absolutely sure that God wanted the children to have ice cream, and it had taken two angels to get the message through.

Why do we who have money for both practical things and luxuries, think that poor people should spend theirs on only practical things? Is that conviction in the Bible somewhere? Does God want only rich children to have ice cream?

The Saint Vincent de Paul shop has made me question many of my convictions in this way. I now know that just because a very logical thought has been in my head for many years, *that is no proof that it is true.*

One day I am visiting Rita, the lady with one eye, sciatica, and fragile diabetes. She doesn't have any money, because she has not yet been able to get approved for disability. Her pro bono lawyer has been working on it, and she hears from him every few months, but there is no telling how much longer the process will take. Because Rita has no income and is living off food stamps, there is no such thing as luxuries unless she can coax a friend into sharing. The St. Vincent de Paul Society has been that sort of friend for Rita, but she does not rely on our generosity alone. She belongs to a church that helps her out from time to time, and she has siblings who live in places like Chicago and Maryland whom she can call on in an emergency. She is also the sort of neighbor in her apartment complex who is willing to share with everyone else and is the occasional recipient of neighborly help. Today I have brought her some necessities such as paper products, detergent, and bus tokens, which can't be purchased with food stamps.

In the course of our conversation, she asks me to drive her to the laundromat. The Laundromat is next door to her apartment, so I figure out pretty quickly that what she is actually asking me for is the money to put into the machines.

We haul the sacks of clothing to my car, and as we load them into the trunk, Rita notices the box of books, which I push to the back, and she asks me what they are. I explain that I have written a book about my experiences volunteering at the thrift store.

"Am I in it?" she asks, reaching in and plucking one out to look at it.

"Of course not," I tell her. "I wouldn't put you in a book without asking you."

"Well, put me in the next one," she says. "Can I read this?" She flips through it.

"Sure."

I latch the trunk, and we hop in the car, drive around to the strip mall next door, and unload again. After we pack everything into two triple-load washers, I drop in the coins.

We settle down in the plastic chairs to wait. While we watch the suds slosh back and forth in the round windows, I tell Rita about losing my wallet and all the trouble it has cost me to replace everything.

She is indignant. "Do you know who it is did it?"

"No," I tell her, "but the police are working on it."

"Well, if I find out who it is, I'll go over to his place and shake it out of him. It's no good letting people get away with that nonsense."

I grin at her. "Well, I hope you don't find out because I don't want you getting in a fight over it. You could get hurt doing stuff like that."

She flaps one hand dismissively. "I can take care of myself. If I find out where he lives, I just need to get in the door. If I was in shape like I used to be, I'd whip his butt." Then she laughs and says, "The other day I almost had to sit on my neighbor to get my stuff back, I tell you!"

I straighten up and look at her with interest. "Really? What happened?"

"Well, that girl, she is such a measly thing, always hanging around her boyfriend and not caring about the rest of the neighbors at all—too far above us. The other day she knocks on my door and says in this whiney voice, 'Rita, can I come over and watch television with you?'"

"I'm thinking, *What's this about*? So I says to her, 'Why don't you watch your own television?'"

"'Oh, my boyfriend went downtown to do some business, and I'm lonely. It's no fun watching TV by myself.'"

"So, I shrugged and let her in, and we sat down and put in a movie and started watching for only about five minutes, and she says she has to use the bathroom. She goes in there and afterwards comes back and sits down. It's not two minutes later, and she says she's sleepy. Off she goes home and I'm sitting there thinking, *Something's not right*. So I go into my bathroom, and if she hasn't stolen my toilet paper, the little weasel! I march over to her place and walk right in the door without knocking, because this is not a time to knock. I says to her, 'What you doing stealing my toilet paper? I was nice enough to invite you into my house and you steal my paper? I would have given you some if you'd of asked. What kind of low person are you?'"

"She had it sitting on the bathroom counter, and I snatched it up and walked back out of there."

I am grinning broadly at this tale, but I am also slightly horrified. I am thinking about the person who stole my wallet and then went on a shopping spree at Wal-Mart.

Did they buy toilet paper?

Does it make a difference what they bought?

My convictions tell me stealing is wrong. And, certainly, Rita's neighbor should have asked for the paper instead of swiping it. But what kind of a system do we have that does not allow a poor family to buy toilet paper with their food stamps? What are we afraid they are going to do—waste it? After all, even ice cream can be purchased with food stamps.

Who are the measly ones in this society?

19

LOOKING AT THE SUN

At 5:40 p.m. every day the Virgin Mother appears to the Medjugorje visionaries.

This does not take place at St. James Church, because the local bishop lacks enthusiasm for this sort of thing and will not allow the building to be used for Mary's apparitions. Mary, though disappointed, indulges the church officials and arranges to appear to the seers where they gather to pray in a private residence, or on the mountain, or even when they travel to other places.

We Kalamazoo pilgrims plan to gather at St. James at five to pray the Rosary before the daily apparition. I arrive at four-forty so I can get a seat this time and avoid kneeling on the stone floor. But I end up giving it to an elderly lady because it is more distracting for me to watch her kneel than it is to feel the ache in my own joints.

At precisely 5:40, the packed church gets quiet, and we all pause and pray silently while the apparition is taking place. Since this happens off-site, the silent pause feels a little odd, but not all that different from most of my prayer life. Every day I talk to God, listen to the silence, talk some more, and listen to more silence. Once in a while this pattern produces comfort during distress and inspiration during a slack period of growth, but mostly I pray because when I *don't* pray, my life doesn't work very well. Simple as that—daily prayer keeps me from backsliding.

Although I admire mystics, it is clear that mysticism is not my charism.

When I was a teenager, I chose Teresa of Ávila for my confirmation saint's name. This sixteenth-century Spanish Carmelite nun enjoyed both a keen sense of the ridiculous and a spectacular prayer life. She conversed with Jesus, had visions and locutions, and experienced miraculous cures of physical ailments. I loved reading her autobiography and her later writings about mystical prayer, but try as I might, my relationship with God has always remained solidly earth-bound. I pray, I go to Mass, light candles, obey most of the rules, exert some effort in acts of charity, and study hard, but God neither talks out loud to me, nor does he make guest appearances.

Mind you, I am not complaining.

God has provided me with excellent loving parents, siblings, spouse, children, and friends. My needs for food, shelter, clothing, education, and health care have been met abundantly throughout my life. I have never been abused, abandoned, or falsely accused. In short—*why would God speak to me?* There are a lot of people who need his attention for basic survival in this world—I understand priorities.

But still, I am drawn to mystics. I would not be in Medjugorje, Bosnia-Herzegovina, if I wasn't pretty darn fascinated with the idea of the Mother of God visiting and talking to people in the flesh.

Crowded together inside St. James, after the time of the apparition passes, the congregation sings some standard, guitar-led Mary songs in Latin and Croatian. Then we resume standing shoulder to shoulder in the back of the church, grateful not to be on our knees. The Mass begins at six. We progress efficiently through the Confiteor, the Old Testament reading, the Psalm, and onto the Gospel. This is all done in Croatian, but that doesn't really matter too much because the Roman Catholic Mass is so reliably standardized that it is easy to tell where we are at all times. Like most Catholics, I have the entire thing memorized anyway, so I spend more time than I should admiring the windows.

After the celebrant finishes reading the Gospel, my wandering attention defaults back to the front when another priest steps up to the ambo and begins reading the same Gospel over again in Italian. When he finishes, yet another steps forward and repeats the reading in Polish. We go through Spanish, English, and Dutch, and I begin seriously to regret giving up my seat in the pew. In all, they read the Gospel in ten different languages before we are allowed to listen to the homily, which is in Croatian. I don't understand the message at all, but that doesn't matter because I am so relieved when they only give it to us once. With the repeated readings and the add-on prayers at the end, we don't get out of there until seven-thirty. Three hours of standing or kneeling on a stone floor in close quarters with fervent, hungry people who have mostly spent the day climbing rocky hills is a tempering sort of experience.

As I file out the side door of the church and head back to our B and B, I am feeling ashamed of my lack of enthusiasm for all these hours of liturgy, prayers, and polyglot Bible readings. I realize I was drawn to this place because of the mystical part, but what I have found is the same familiar religion I have at home.

Essentially the same, but here in Medjugorje everything is more so.

I admire the way these people in this town have centered their community around God, Mary, prayer, and the Mass. They pray the rosary every day. They go to Mass every day. They frequently confess their sins, open their homes to strangers, give alms, and study the Scriptures. And they do this while a vicious war is pounding the hills all around them.

It feels as if I've stepped into the Middle Ages.

Or perhaps . . . could I have stepped into the future?

This is a strange idea, so I quickly shrug it off as I continue on my way to my very delayed supper. As I walk around the side of St. James, I pass a stone wall where two of my fellow pilgrims from Kalamazoo are seated side by side. They are facing the setting sun and exclaiming over the colors, hugging each other with their adjacent arms, pointing in wide arcs with their free hands, and smiling joyfully.

I stop walking when I see their excitement and look over my shoulder to where they are pointing. The sun is about two sphere widths over the horizon in a cloudless sky. I immediately raise my hand, shading my eyes to block out the intensity of the low-angled light. To me, it looks like the same sun we see in Michigan. I turn back to my companions and hold my palms up in a silent question.

"Don't you see it?" they say in excitement. "It's twirling in circles—and the colors are gorgeous! Isn't it beautiful?"

I look again, of course.

But, alas, it is boringly consistent with the sun I have always seen. My hand goes reflexively to shade my eyes. I turn back to the two on the wall, and I am suddenly struck by the fact that they are looking wide-eyed at this brilliant sphere without the help of sunglasses or hat brims. Their hands are neither shading their eyes nor blocking the light that is shining on their faces with a direct glare. They aren't even squinting.

How can they do that? Surely, they will fry their retinas to ashes.

I look over my shoulder yet again, but I cannot prevent my hand from blocking the intense light.

"Don't you see it?" they ask me excitedly.

I shake my head. "It looks like the sun to me."

They look at me in puzzlement, then continue chattering with each other, exclaiming about their shared vision, telling me not to worry, that perhaps if I watch awhile, I will see it, too.

But I am a little too disappointed to sit quietly and hope. I shrug my shoulders, turn away, and head toward our hostel. As I walk along the road, I pass other people who are not seeing anything to exclaim over in the sky, but there are also a couple of unshuttered faces along the way:

people who are soaking up a vision I can't see, that I can't even look toward.

As I pass them, I am suddenly struck by a realization. *If we all could look at the sun dancing in the sky with unreal colors, then it would be merely a phenomena. But because only a few can see it, then it is instead a gift given to them. And the folks like me, who cannot see it? We are the proof that something unique happened for them alone.*

That's a pretty nice gift.

20

CHRISTMAS ANGELS

In the late fall we always have a run on men's gloves at the St. Vincent de Paul shop. Homeless people don't have a place to store last year's winter garments, so when those first freezing temperatures hit, our sidewalk neighbors come asking for something to cover their hands.

In November, Fran, one of our volunteers, puts her head into the office and says, "Jane, don't we have any men's gloves stored away somewhere?"

"Sorry," I answer, "We ran out of them in less than a week this year."

There are two reasons for this: first, it is below freezing in Michigan during most of November, and second, all the churches in town have coat, mitten, and hat drives at Christmastime. This makes no sense at all.

People who live in our town are all wearing cold weather gear themselves long before December 25, but when they organize charity drives for these necessities, they do it around a liturgical holiday that falls in the dead of winter. St. Vincent de Paul will be flooded with coats and mittens the week before Christmas, and meanwhile, the poor people are sticking their bare hands in the pockets of their light-weight jackets and finding it hard to give thanks at Thanksgiving.

Fran looks distressed at the news about the gloves, but then a determined look comes over her face. She pulls on her coat and goes out the back door, coming back seconds later with a pair of men's leather gloves. She pats them fondly and says, "These were my late husband's, and I've been using them to brush the snow off the car, but I'm sure he would have wanted me to give them away if someone else needed them."

She walks out onto the sales floor and hands them to a young man, saying, "I'll pray for you."

He smiles. "I believe in God, and I thank you for your prayers."

The following week, Fran and two of our other volunteers get tired of telling cold people that we can't help them, so they hand me cash from their purses with instructions to go buy as many gloves and socks as the money will cover.

I drive out of town to a discount store that sells cheap imported items and find insulated gloves at fifteen dollars a dozen. They also have knit caps and packs of socks marked to a fraction of the price our homeless friends would find within walking distance of their shelter.

As I drive back to St. Vincent de Paul, I grow unusually nostalgic thinking about Henry Ford, a Michigan icon. One hundred years ago his idea was to pay his workers enough so they could purchase the automobiles they were building—a simple but revolutionary way of doing business that helped create the American middle class.

In today's weird economy, poor people in third-world countries make products so cheaply that middle-class people in America can give them away to poor people here who can't get jobs because the jobs moved to the third-world countries. I start to grow nostalgic thinking about the United Auto Workers (UAW), another Michigan icon. Henry Ford would have begged to differ with me on this, but I suspect these two old enemies needed each other more than they realized.

I arrive back at St. Vincent de Paul and pull up next to the Dumpster in my usual parking spot. The lid of the Dumpster is flung wide open. We don't leave it that way—anonymous visitors do. As I step out of my car, one of these visitors pokes his head up out of the metal container. He has his hands full of chipped ceramics and silk flowers.

"Good morning," I tell him. What else does one say to a person standing in a Dumpster?

"Morning!" he answers cheerfully. "It sure is a cold one."

"Yes," I agree.

He holds up an angel figurine to show me. "Isn't that pretty?"

His hands are chapped and red with the cold and I am thinking more about the gloves in my trunk than about the angel. "Yes, it is. Aren't your hands freezing?"

He shrugs. "I don't want to rip my gloves in here. There's always broken glass, so I have to be careful, or I'll get a hole in them."

I walk around to the back of my car, open the trunk, and pull out one pair of men's gloves. Reaching over the side of the Dumpster, I hand them to my neighbor. "Take these and see if they fit," I tell him.

He shakes his head in refusal. "Those are too nice to use in here. My hands will warm up as soon as I'm done."

Using a little persuasion, I talk him into putting the new gloves in his pockets and using his old ones for his search, explaining that we don't want him to cut himself and get blood all over our Dumpster. He can see the logic of that and accepts the gloves with many thanks.

"What are you looking for?" I ask.

"I want to find a Christmas gift for my mom, but I guess I'm done. I think she'll love this angel, don't you?"

When I walk back into the shop, I'm told a man is waiting for me. It is Otis, the downhearted fellow to whom I had given the twenty dollars to take the kids to McDonald's. When I greet him, he says earnestly, "Did you get the presents I left for you?"

I don't know what he is talking about, but he explains that he and his girlfriend were so grateful for the money I had given him that they wanted to thank me with some small gifts. He says that he had left them with the person in the office the previous day. We walk in there, and sure enough, several wrapped packages are on the side table.

I remonstrate with him about such unnecessary extravagance, but he only smiles and urges me to open the presents. I can see that he sincerely wants to do this, so I unwrap the packages one at a time and exclaim over each. There is a votive candleholder with "Hope" spelled on the outside, a small resin cross that quotes Philippians: "I have strength for everything through him who empowers me," and a pair of drugstore reading glasses.

Otis must have spent half the money I had given him to buy these items. I am embarrassed but very touched, so I stand up and give him a hug. Then I call some of my fellow volunteers into the office to show off Otis's wonderful generosity. They praise and compliment the gifts, and we all make a general fuss over him.

We, of course, tell him he should not be spending any money on us, that there is no need to thank us in this way. It is close to Christmas. He should be saving money to buy gifts for his own loved ones.

He admits that Christmas may be a problem this year because he and his girlfriend are still struggling to come up with the rent to stave off eviction.

Peggy says to me, "Can't we sign up Otis for one of our Christmas baskets?"

Of course we can. It is a couple weeks early to be doing this, but this man obviously qualifies, so we pull out the paperwork and ask him to fill in the details about the members of the household, including the children's genders and ages so we will have enough toys available in appropriate categories. I assign him a date and time to come back the week before Christmas so that he can pick out the gifts himself. He walks out, smiling and pleased, a much different picture from the last time he had visited our store.

We are all pleased. I leave the little cross in the office and take the candleholder home to place in my living room. I'm not sure what to do with the reading glasses; they are not my prescription, but he couldn't have known that.

21

ALL HEAVEN BREAKING LOOSE

At the St. Vincent de Paul Thrift Shop we have a few rules, and mostly we find it difficult to stick to them. But a charity can't run without rules, or the word will get around that we are easy targets for knaves, and then all hell breaks loose, when what we are *trying* to encourage is all heaven breaking lose.

One thing we are firm about is that people to whom we have promised financial assistance must show us all their promissory notes from other churches and agencies so we can verify that they have collected the necessary funds to pay their bill in full. It's no good paying only part of what's due on an eviction notice because the landlord can take the partial payment and still evict at will. That means we have succeeded in helping the landlord but we have not helped our friend in need. Which is not our goal.

I am explaining this rule to one of our clients, and she purses her lips and says, "You're telling me that I have to run around town to a bunch of churches and get them to promise me money and after that, I need to run around *again* and show everyone what everyone else promised?"

"Yes."

"Can't I phone you?"

"We need to see the notes and receipts."

"A fax?"

"You can try that, but our fax machine isn't reliable—it's a castoff that was donated."

"E-mail?"

"Sorry, we don't have Internet."

She flings up her hands. "What a crazy way to run a charity! Who owns this place?"

I think a moment. No one has ever asked me this question before. "Well, um . . . God does, I guess."

This time her eyes actually bulge. "*God*? Did you say *God*?"

I feel apologetic. "See, we're all volunteers, and our group owns the building, but the church owns the land it's on, so I guess . . . yeah—put it all together and God must own the charity."

It looks for a moment as if she might start shouting, but she doesn't. She stares at me, taking in what I have said, and then—she starts to chuckle.

"Okay, well. If God owns this place, then I guess I'll just have to follow His rules, won't I?"

As she leaves with her good humor and her wad of paper promises, I wonder if God would really approve of these rules. If it's true that the St. Vincent de Paul Thrift Shop is his place, then he sure has some amateurish workers running it for him. Half the time we pile rule upon rule, and half the time we throw them all out the window (like the time I gave Otis the twenty) in the interest of piling on love instead.

Since love is the goal, what can possibly go wrong?

I am having lunch with my friend Becky when her cell phone begins to buzz. She excuses herself to check it, just in case the text message is from one of her children. She looks at the screen and sighs. "Oh, it's only my cousin sending me Scripture verses again. She does that all the time, but lately she's been really piling them on. It feels like she's trying to convert me."

Becky is one of those friends with whom the conversation almost always turns to God. At this moment we are in the middle of discussing what it means to live by faith and the excruciating uncertainty that often requires of us. It's a lively, openhearted exchange we are having, and then this interruption. Does Becky really need these scriptural reminders? Or is it actually her cousin who needs to give them?

While interviewing an out-of-work carpenter at the St. Vincent de Paul store, the young man tells me about all the long months of doing odd jobs and worrying about the bills. I sympathize with him over the state of the economy while I fill out the form for assistance with an eviction. He is thinking of moving to Florida for the hurricane season in order to be on the spot for insurance work in the aftermath of a storm. His brother is already down there, waiting hopefully for a weather catastrophe. Before this young man leaves the state, he wants to be squared away with the rent he owes his patient landlord, so he is here to apply for our assistance.

I hand him a promissory note for his rent and ask if I may give him a prayer card, too. He thanks me for the money and puts his hand out for the card.

He glances at it briefly and looks relieved. "Thank you for not giving me the Serenity Prayer," he says.

I can't help but laugh. "I take it you have that one already?"

He nods. "A person can't ask for help without getting it pressed into their hand. I'm kinda tired of it. It's nothing against prayer. I do that already. And serenity is fine, but what I really need is a job."

As he leaves, I muse that there is nothing intrinsically wrong with the Serenity Prayer, and there is nothing wrong with Becky's cousin sending Scripture verses. What I have to remember is that sometimes, it makes a better gift if I *say* prayers for people rather than *hand* them to people.

22

VICKA

Breakfast is at seven every day in Medjugorje, and after several days, the menu of cold bologna, cheese, and oranges is getting a bit old. Apparently Martha is tired of it too, and she announces as we gather around the table that she has requested omelets this morning. Several jars of peanut butter are slipped gratefully into backpacks, and we bow our heads for the meal grace. It is pronounced with even more exuberance than usual by Fr. Daryl.

While we wait for the omelets, Martha tells us that at seven-forty-five we will be walking to one of the visionary's homes. Vicka is the oldest of the visionaries, and she not only talks with the Virgin Mother every day but also spends hours speaking with groups of pilgrims from all over the world. The life of a mystic is not an easy one. This young woman's time is devoted to God, to prayer, and to answering the same questions over and over again every single day. Martha informs us that if we want the Virgin Mother to bless any religious items we have, Martha will give them to Vicka, and Our Lady's blessing will be requested at today's apparition.

In my pocket is the rosary I bought for Dorothy, so I give that to Martha. When I purchased it from a little store in the town, the shopkeeper gave me a big hug for my attempts at Croatian and then told me she was a Muslim refugee from Zagreb. It somehow pleases me that the Virgin Mary will be blessing a rosary bought from a Muslim and given to a Catholic. I think Dorothy will like that.

As Martha collects all our rosaries, medals, and holy cards into a plastic sack, she drops some odd information into the conversation. It seems that even though Mary will happily bless our sacramentals, she insists that it will still be necessary to have them blessed again by a priest. "Mine is only a mother's blessing," Mary has told the seers. "A priestly blessing is still important."

This seems so absurd to me that it must be true. Only the Virgin Mother herself could come up with a statement as meek and humble as that one.

While we ponder this and jot down our prayer petitions, which we will give to Vicka, our hostess and her daughter walk into the room proudly bearing enormous platters. They present each of us with our own individually prepared omelet, amidst cheers of "puno hvala!" Everyone has learned how to say thank you by now, and it is most sincerely spoken this morning.

As we pick up our forks, I ask Martha what she has planned for the afternoon and learn we will be on our own. This sounds fine by me. It looks like it will be good weather, and I would like to climb Mount Krizevac by myself without the distraction of the group. I would not be on this pilgrimage except for Martha and Fr. Daryl's willingness to organize and lead it, so I feel a little guilty about wanting some space apart.

I feel guilty because I am becoming aware that God *likes* groups.

Sure, he loves us individually, as a father loves a child, but he also seems to have a penchant for big gatherings of his children. This little town is a wonderful example of how he works in our world. It is located in a country composed of Muslims, Catholics, and Orthodox who have a long tradition of not getting along together very well and are currently trying their best to kill each other. It would have been much simpler for God if he had sent Mary to a place where various religious groups live in harmony and peace. A place like . . .

Well, okay—maybe Medjugorje is as good a place as any.

But you would think that he would at least bring pilgrims here who enjoy packed churches, language barriers, and cold showers. People like . . . *not me.*

But he didn't. He brought me.

And this morning I am tired of the crowded togetherness, the half-understood conversations, and bologna for breakfast. So I am determined to break loose from the community and take off on my own this afternoon, and I feel my spirits lift at the thought.

I cheerfully sink my fork into the eggs and taste my first mouthful of—bologna omelet.

After breakfast we walk to Vicka's house, which is like every other house in the village. We wouldn't have found it on our own without a guide because there are no plaques or sightseeing arrows to indicate that one of the visionaries resides here. The only distinguishing feature is the seventy-five Italians crowded onto and around her front porch.

It is raining again, so we hunch under our plastic ponchos and stand in the narrow street, trying to keep our place as other pilgrims pack in around us.

After fifteen minutes Vicka appears at the top of the porch steps behind a small balcony railing. She has a smile that doesn't stop—ever. She speaks through an interpreter to the Italians for ten or fifteen minutes, beaming at them the whole time. When she is finished, the Italians hold up cameras and rosary beads in equal numbers. Vicka joyfully motions for them to leave and they reluctantly give way to those of us standing in the street.

Now it is our turn to pack ourselves onto the porch, and under my breath I promise God that when I return home, I will thank my parish priest for the amazing gift of kneelers and weatherproof roofs.

Close-up, Vicka's smiling face is exponentially more beautiful than her smiling face from forty feet away.

I learn that *joy* is not a frivolous word.

I forget about the rain dripping down my neck as I strain to hear the English-language interpreter who is translating this young woman's simple words. Her message from the Virgin Mary is that we should pray for young people. Apparently Mary is anxious about the youth in the world and how they are coping.

When Vicka is finished with her little talk, she tells us she wants to pray for each of us individually, and in order to do that she will look into each of our faces. The interpreter asks us to shuffle around in the tight space so that Vicka has a clear view of every single person. We all do this, and then she begins with those on the left, smiling into each one's eyes by turns from her perch at the top of the steps, whispering prayers to herself. As she takes this extended time, the crowd becomes completely still, the cameras are lowered, and all of us are absorbed in watching this systematically grace-filled blessing.

When it is my turn and her eyes reach out to mine, I have trouble holding her gaze. There is something difficult about looking directly into love. I want to glance away in embarrassment, but I don't. I return her empathetic smile with a helpless question written on my face. Her mouth forms words in Croatian, and it is over. She turns to my neighbor, and I gratefully let my gaze drop.

After several minutes she finishes, and we are dismissed like the Italians were because another crowd, whose members speak one of the other major languages, has formed behind us in the street. Vicka's morning is mapped out for her.

I make my way off the porch, thinking about intercessory prayer in a whole new light. I don't believe, during my entire life, that I have ever prayed for someone while looking directly into their eyes.

Quite the opposite.

Typically, if I am praying for someone who is actually present, both of us will keep our eyes completely shut, or our heads bowed, or both. Even priests raise one hand and place their attention on the words in the book. I have never before experienced anything like Vicka's praying.

Paradoxically, her praying for us individually has made us become more of a group by our sharing in this extraordinary experience. We walk through the sodden streets reciting together the Joyful Mysteries on our rosary beads for the sake of all the young people in the world.

And the prayer really is joyful.

23

DOROTHY

Dorothy is the volunteer at St. Vincent de Paul who is responsible for my being a Vincentian. She invited me to join and taught me the mechanics of working in a charity that has nobody clearly in charge. She patiently ignored my efforts to improve everyone else, and wisely encouraged my attempts to improve myself.

I do not see her regularly anymore because we work on different days, but occasionally we go out for lunch and catch up. Because she is such a good listener, I always enjoy our conversations.

I do recognize the problem with this statement.

I know that I need to develop a capacity for listening—the kind of empathetic listening that Dorothy is so good at. During our get-togethers I try to figure out what it is that she does differently from most people I know, and I come to some vague conclusions. Talking to Dorothy is like talking with someone out of a nineteenth-century novel. It is as if she grew up with the March sisters in *Little Women* and learned manners from Marmee.

When we meet at the diner, she greets me with a small wave and says something like, "What a lovely idea to meet here, Jane. I've been looking forward to our lunch all week."

"It's wonderful to see you, too," I tell her. "Where would you like to sit?"

"You pick," she says. "How are your daughters? Has Ellen graduated? Is Martha still working at the library?"

"Yes, Ellen graduated and now she is looking for a job. You know how much Martha loves books—the library is perfect for her. Here's the menu. I hope there is something you like."

"I like everything. I will put Ellen on my prayer list. And Dean? Is his business doing all right in this economy? Tell me how he is."

You get the idea.

I try my best to say something earnest, and she always trumps me. And none of this is artificial. She is sincerely lovely, and I love to be around her. Like spending time in Medjugorje, spending time with Dorothy feels like a step back to another, more civilized era . . . or is it a step forward?

It is a great shock the morning I walk into the thrift store and find the other volunteers are collecting money to send flowers to Dorothy.

She has broken her hip.

My heart sinks. A broken hip is often the beginning of the end for very elderly people, so I begin to brace myself for deteriorating reports of her condition.

It is a couple of weeks before I find out where she is and go to visit her.

At the assisted-living home she has a pleasant room that is decorated with photos of her family and vases of cut flowers. An aluminum walker is next to her chair, and she is wearing thick socks that she seems embarrassed about. I bend down to give her a peck on the cheek and sit down in a chair across from hers. She asks about my daughters and about Dean's business.

I pass on get-well wishes from the other volunteers, and then she says, "I feel terrible to have left you shorthanded like this. I'm working hard in physical therapy so I can come back to work, but they won't tell me how long it might take. It's even difficult to get a straight answer out of my doctor about when I can go home."

I don't want to encourage hopes that might not be realistic, so I change the subject. "How did you break your hip? Did you fall at home? Was anyone with you?"

She laughs a little. "It was silly, really. I went on one of those bus trips through the Senior Center. It was a trip to Greenfield Village and the Henry Ford Museum in Dearborn. I hadn't been there in years, so I thought it would be a fun day, and it was. But at the very end, when I was getting on the bus to come home, I stumbled and fell, but not hard. I caught myself a little with my hands, but I didn't want to break my wrist again, so I landed on my hip, too. Well, everyone rushed over and picked me up, and I was fine—really—mostly just shaken. I was embarrassed by all the fuss, so I just climbed onto the bus and found my seat, and pretty soon everyone left me alone. But by the time we arrived back in Kalamazoo, everything had stiffened up a bit, and you know—I couldn't even stand up to get myself off the bus. Isn't that silly?"

I purse my lips. "You broke your hip and then rode two hours home on a bus?"

She waves her hand mildly. "It wasn't much of a bother until the last hour."

No matter what the doctors and physical therapists may think, it sounds to me like this ninety-something lady will be back to work at the thrift shop someday soon. Kindness and endurance always attract God's grace.

And I am right. Within six months, Dorothy is behind the cash register again. I still have so much to learn from her, and God, apparently, knows that.

24

Asking God for Answers

My aunt Kay, a kindergarten teacher, used to observe, "Children who hang on to their belief in Santa Claus find it easy to be Catholics later on in life."

Both stances require a faith in wonderful things.

The mystery of the grown man dressed in red who flies around the neighborhood giving away toys, attracts us just like the baby born in the manger who grows up to defeat all the big meanies and takes us with him to live happily forever after.

Children and Catholics both love superheroes.

At St. Vincent de Paul we love Christmas. Helping the poor would be a harder job if we didn't allow ourselves to participate in this great banish-the-darkness feast. Sure, people need money for utility bills and eviction notices, but just like they need ice cream in the summer, they also need to celebrate the birth of Jesus when winter is pelting our optimism. So every year we make up Christmas baskets for some of our neighbors. And every year, to help with this project, the Sunday-school children of St. Joseph Parish in Kalamazoo generously give us mittens, scarves, and toys.

The week before Christmas, while I am sorting their bags of gifts, one of the items I pull out is a Spider-Man winter coat. This isn't something I can put with the mittens and scarves, and it doesn't fit on the toy table, either. But it is brand-new with all the tags still attached. There are more than seventy-five kids on our list, and we have begun to fret that there won't be enough toys, so I set the coat aside as a last resort—for when we run out of the good stuff.

The Christmas-basket project at our St. Vinnie's works like this. We divide the items into age-appropriate groups on tables in our storage room. Then we schedule appointments for the parents to come to the store to choose what their children will enjoy. When they have made all their selections, we sit Mom and Dad down with a cup of coffee and holiday cookies, and our volunteers wrap each of the gifts in festive paper. We chat with the parents, asking how we should address the gift tags: *from Mom or Dad? From baby Jesus? From Santa?* Whatever they prefer, that's what we write.

On the basket giveaway day, I am working at the desk in the same room where all this wrapping and chatting are going on. My job is to organize the lists of families, check them off when they come in, and hand them a Christmas card with a gift certificate from a local grocery store enclosed so they can purchase food extras for a Christmas dinner. While I am sorting through applications and envelopes, trying to keep everything in order, the phone rings. It is the police detective from the City of Portage, who has been working on the case of my stolen wallet.

He tells me they have an identification of the person who used my credit cards. Because I was able to give them the information from the banks and the credit card companies, the detective was able to go to the stores and review the security-camera tapes, pinpointing the customer who used my cards.

He has two questions for me: Do I know a person named Quentin Conway? And did I give this man permission to use my credit cards?

I answer negatively to both questions, and the policeman thanks me and says he will keep in touch.

I hang up the phone, my mind now thoroughly distracted. *Well. That's probably a good thing that they have identified the thief . . . but I don't have time to think about it right now because this is Christmas-basket day at St. Vinnie's and I have a lot of work to do.* I keep thinking about it anyway.

The store is crowded with volunteers and customers, people coming and going, the crackling of wrapping paper, the smells of coffee and peppermint candy, the phone and the cash register ringing, and the general excitement of the approaching holiday.

I love this stuff. I am not going to let that old stolen-wallet stress interfere with one of my favorite days of the year.

I firmly set aside the conversation with the policeman and go back to the list of applications in front of me, sorting them into chronological order for today's appointments. When the pile is organized, I look at the top application and read the name of the next person we will be helping.

Quentin Otis Conway.

I read it again.

It says the same thing.

Part of the form is in my handwriting. I filled it in six weeks ago.

I glance around quickly and see Elizabeth wrapping packages with three other volunteers at the pricing table. I signal to her to come to me. She gives me a curious look, puts aside what she is doing, and weaves her way across the room. I hand her the application and ask, "Is this Otis's family? The guy who gave me the little presents? Do you remember?"

Elizabeth takes it into her hand, looks it over briefly, and nods. "Of course, I remember. He lives one block over—with his girlfriend and the four kids. What's up?"

"I didn't know his first name was Quentin."

She looks again at the paper in her hand. "I guess I didn't know that either. He always goes by Otis when he's in here. And he's here almost every other day to ask for one thing or another. He's getting to be a bit of pest. But Quentin or Otis—that's his address all right."

I take the application back in my hand and read it silently.

Elizabeth tips her head sideways, studying me. "What are you thinking?"

I tell her about the amazing coincidence that the person the police have identified as the suspect who used my credit cards is also named Quentin Conway.

Elizabeth snatches the application back from me, reads it, and says, "He's coming in here in twenty minutes!"

"Do you think they could be the same Quentin Conway?"

Elizabeth has seen me in this state before, so she doesn't waste time arguing this point with me. "What are you going to do?"

"Giving him a Christmas basket would be the ultimate irony. He bought a hundred Christmases with my credit cards already."

She winces. "True. But the baskets are for the kids—not for him."

I put my elbows on the desk and put my face in my hands. "I don't know what to do. All I know is, I don't want to talk to him right now. It's too weird."

She looks steadily at me for a moment and then says, "You can leave, Jane. We have enough volunteers here to handle everything. If you want to go, no one would blame you."

I glance at the clock. *Fifteen minutes before his appointment.*

I stand up, pull my coat off the back of the chair, and feel for the car keys in the pocket. I give Elizabeth a quick hug as I hand her the stack of applications, and tell her not to mention to anyone why I have left. Amidst all the hubbub in the store, I slip unnoticed out the side door and walk toward my car.

When I reach it, I stop and stare at all the cars jammed into our little parking lot. It's the busiest day of the year at

St. Vinnie's, and I hate to leave all the commotion on the shoulders of the other volunteers.

But I really can't face Otis right now.

Across the parking lot, past the school, about a block away, I can see the steeple of the cathedral. I jam my hands into my coat pockets and walk in that direction, not sure why or what I'm going to do when I get there.

It's a brisk day, and my hat and mittens are in my car, but I keep trudging toward the church. When I reach it, I am cold, so I decide to try the door on the off chance that it is unlocked. By some miracle it is. I slip inside. The place is empty, the only movement the flickering of a few candles. I sit down in a pew near the front and let the warmth of the building soak into my chilled ears and fingers.

While I sit there, I ask God a few questions.

I ask him why Otis would steal from me and then continue to come back again and again to ask for charity.

God doesn't answer that question.

I ask God what I have done to deserve this kind of treatment.

We continue on with the Godlike silence.

I ask if I am supposed to go back and forgive Otis. Tell him I know he is the thief. Demand an apology. Renege on the Christmas basket.

As usual, I hear nothing from God, but in my memory appear the young woman's instructions: *Don't try to save that person; that's not your job. God saves people.*

I ask God if these instructions are from him, or am I only fooling myself.

No answer to that one either.

I feel myself growing angry. It's one thing to be robbed. It's another to be robbed by someone who pretends to appreciate me and the work we do at St. Vincent de Paul. My jaw tightens, and the church is annoyingly quiet. Or maybe it is God who is annoyingly quiet. Hard to tell which.

Okay. I've been Catholic long enough to recognize some temptations when they appear. Anger, agitation, and a general loss of peace are not usually part of God's modus operandi. Some other type of spiritual entity might be answering my questions. I pull down the kneeler, plop forward onto it, and say the prayer to St. Michael the archangel:

> St. Michael the Archangel,
> defend us in the day of battle.
> Be our safeguard against the wickedness and snares of the
>   devil.
> May God rebuke him, we humbly pray;
> And do Thou, O Prince of the Heavenly Host—
> by the Divine Power of God—
> cast into hell, Satan and all the evil spirits
> who roam about the world seeking the ruin of souls.

I repeat this about half a dozen times. That helps. The anger subsides a bit.

I sit back down and look at the crucifix in front of me. My jaw is now relaxed, and the unanswered questions seem beside the point, so I don't go back to them.

Instead, I ask God, *What am I supposed to do now?*

The silence stretches, so I let it. There is no call to action in it but no anger, either, so I sit tight, exactly where I am.

I didn't really expect an answer anyway. I am no mystic.

After a little while, it occurs to me that today is the busiest day of the year at St. Vinnie's, and not only that—it is my favorite day of the year in the store.

I should be there.

Otis is not the one who should be there. *I am the one who should be there.* That is simply clear. It is the only clear thing about this situation.

Still not knowing what I am going to do or say when I see Otis, still feeling enormously uncomfortable with the coming encounter, I stand up and head for the door.

25

THERE ARE MANY GIFTS

There are varieties of gifts, but the same Spirit; and there are varieties of services, but the same Lord.
—1 CORINTHIANS 12:4–5

I walk in the front door of the store and instantly spot Otis talking with Peggy in the sorting room. There is nothing to do but walk toward them. I am almost there when Elizabeth steps out from the office, grabs my arm and says, "I'm glad you're back. There's a woman here who needs extra help selecting the gifts for her kids. She's sight-impaired, so someone will have to describe each gift to her. Can you do it?"

"Um . . . sure," I say, and Elizabeth hands me the list of children in the family, tugging me toward the lady with the white cane sitting at the lunch table. We move past Peggy and Otis, who both smile at me.

Otis says, "Hi, Jane. How have you been? I haven't seen you in awhile."

I glance at Peggy, who says, "What happened? Someone said you left."

I say, "Hi, Otis," and Elizabeth ushers me straight past them.

Elizabeth pulls me over to the lunch table and introduces me to a smiling lady who chatters at me enthusiastically about how wonderful it is to be at St. Vincent de Paul today. She goes on for several minutes, and I feel myself becoming calmer while listening to her. When I suggest we begin selecting the gifts, she stands up, tucks her cane under her arm, and puts her hand on my offered elbow. We walk together up the short ramp to the storage room, where the toys are arranged, and there, ahead of us are Peggy and Otis.

Peggy says to me, "We've already finished with the stocking stuffers, Jane, so why don't you start there?"

I escort my charge to the shelves of small toys and explain to her that we will fill a stocking for each of her three children. When I begin to tell her which toys we have to choose from, she asks me to describe every pack of crayons, every coloring book, every detail of the small stuffed animals, and every pattern on the pencils and erasers. She is an attentive mother and takes great pleasure in selecting the items each of her children will enjoy most. Her precise questions require my unwavering, nonstop attention. Peggy and Otis blur into the background while I focus on the shape of butterfly wings, the difficulty level of word-search puzzles, and the color names in a forty-eight-pack box of crayons.

By the time we move on to the larger toys, games, mittens, scarves, and hats, Peggy and Otis have finished, and they leave us alone in the room.

Thank you, Jesus!

It requires a full thirty minutes for us to finish selecting all the gifts, and by the time we are done, I am in love with this lady who sees nothing herself, yet has taught me to look beyond my troubles in order to see every detail of every small thing. I hug her gratefully and turn her over to the crew of volunteers who will wrap the gifts, and then I retreat to the storage room.

Peggy is there alone, a curious smile on her face. "It got crazy busy for a while there. Where did you disappear to?" she asks.

I tell her. And I tell her why, too.

As she listens, a diametrically different kind of smile slowly appears on her face. "Wait. You knew about this? *And we still gave him a Christmas basket?*"

"Who could have seen that coming?" I ask.

"Still—" she concedes, then flings up her hands. "He's *way* too bold. What are you going to do now?"

I shrug. "Let the police handle it, I guess. It's out of my hands at this point."

She nods and looks sober. "Will the police arrest him before Christmas? He seemed genuinely excited about spending the day with the children, and he picked out all their gifts so carefully."

"I don't think so. The Portage police officer said that they need to get a warrant first, and then the Kalamazoo police will have to pick him up because he lives in Kalamazoo. I don't have any idea how long that sort of thing takes, but Christmas is this weekend, so it will probably be after that."

We ponder that for a moment, then Peggy says. "He wanted all the tags to read 'From Otis.'"

"Not from their mom, too? Not even Santa?"

She shakes her head. "Not 'Dad,' either. Every single one was 'From Otis.' And you know how we give a blanket to each child? He asked if he could have an extra one for himself. I said we couldn't do that because we don't have enough of them."

"This has got to be one of the strangest situations I have ever been in."

Just as I finish saying this, Otis appears at the top of the ramp and walks into the room. I don't know what my face looks like, but Peggy's is authentically startled.

Otis says to Peggy, "When I got home, I counted everything, and you mistakenly left out one of the blankets from my bag, so I came back to get it."

I am standing next to the table with the blankets, so Peggy turns and looks at me, her eyebrows raised in a question. Otis walks toward me, his hand out, repeating the request.

Without a word, I reach behind me, pick up a blanket and hold it out to him. He takes it, thanks us, and leaves.

I watch him go and Peggy follows him, closing the door behind him. She turns and says to me, "Since you didn't argue with him, I decided to let it be."

"This situation creeps me out," I admit.

"Perfectly understandable."

The door swings open again, and Elizabeth joins us in the empty room with her jaw set. "Otis asked Walter for some money to keep his electricity from being shut off." Walter is our volunteer handling the utility assistance today. "He told him that we've helped him enough already."

"Walter knows what's going on?" I ask.

"You got a problem with that? When I saw the guy coming back through the door after we just sent him out with four bags of toys—well that's just uncalled for."

Peggy and I nod our heads in agreement. The three of us look at each other with a complexity of emotions on our faces, futilely attempting to absorb the irony of a Christmas morning full of new toys and no heat in the house.

At least they have more than enough blankets.

But we can't worry about that now. We still have a whole slew of other people coming in who need our help providing a celebration of the birth of Christ for their children.

The three of us reopen the door and resume pushing back on the darkness that has crept into the little thrift shop in Kalamazoo. The rest of the afternoon we help parents select toys and hats and blankets until the tables are almost empty. There are only two families left.

The next-to-last mom is looking over the scant selection when she spots the Spider-Man coat behind the table. She reaches for it and says, "Oh, my little boy *loves* Spider-Man. This will be perfect for him, and look—*it's just his size!*"

"What are the chances?" I ask Peggy later, after I tell her this story. We are standing in the empty shop, ready, at last, to go home.

"It's nothing to do with chance," she says.

I have just locked the front door, and we are leaning on the checkout counter, mulling over the day. And there is a lot to mull. While we reflect on thieves, blindness, and Spider-Man, we notice a young man pull up on a bicycle on the other side of the plate-glass door. He is swathed in layers of clothing and scarves, which is good—it's twenty degrees outside. He leans his bike up against the window and reaches for the door handle.

I step up close to the glass and shout, "We're closed. Come back in the morning."

He waves a gloved hand at the basket on his bike and shouts back, "I've got a donation. Will you take it?"

Peggy and I look at each other and sigh. It can't be much of donation if it's in a bike basket, but then again, it couldn't have been easy to ride that bike in this weather.

I pull out my keys and open the door. The young man hands me four sample size bars of soap with labels that read "Super 8."

He says, "I wanted to thank you folks for putting me up in that motel a couple of days last week. I would have been on the street if you hadn't helped. None of the shelters would let me stay in them because I have this infection that's drug resistant. I understand they can't risk everybody else's health, but I was in trouble if you hadn't come through for me." He shoves his hands back inside his coat and shrugs at the little soaps. "Anyway, I just wanted to thank you by making a donation, that's all."

"Where are you staying now?" I ask.

"I found an apartment not far from here. Moved in yesterday. I'm fine—thanks for asking."

Both Peggy and I put our Super 8 soaps on the windowsills in our kitchens. I keep the votive candleholder that reads "Hope" just in case I need it as evidence in court. The reading glasses I donate to the Lions Club. The little ceramic cross, with the Scripture verse from Philippians, "I have strength for everything through him who empowers me," continues to puzzle me. It is still sitting on the shelf in the office at St. Vincent de Paul.

All these things remind me that "there are different spiritual gifts but the same Spirit; there are different forms of service but the same Lord."

And they remind me that it will be amazing grace if I ever figure this out.

26

CLIMBING THE MOUNTAIN ALONE

At last, I have an unscheduled afternoon, and I am determined to climb Mount Krizevac all by myself. Well, not actually by myself, because there are scores of people going up and down all day long, but at least I intend to do it without the distraction of conversation or of helping less fit companions over the rocks. I strap on my tennis shoes, tie my jacket around my waist, and I am on my way without all the delays or head counts that go along with traveling in a large group. I have also decided to attempt the bread-and-water fast that the Virgin Mother has recommended twice per week, so my stomach is grumbling a bit, but that doesn't really bother me.

When I reach the first station of the cross, the angle of the sun is such that it shines past the brass plaque directly into my eyes. I have to move up to within two feet of the large depiction before I can make out the image. This feels a little too close to both the icon and the other climbers. But it is either this culturally uncomfortable encroachment on my personal space, or a dazzling glare, so I crowd in next to the other pilgrims and mumble the prescribed prayers under my breath.

As soon as I finish, I take off up the path, quickly putting distance between myself and the others. This sun-reflection problem occurs over and over again as I climb, so I repeat the pattern of crowding in close to strangers and then dashing off alone. It isn't long before I am breathing very hard and my head begins to pound.

Well, this is a silly way to pray.

But I don't change my methods, and the headache grows worse with every station. Somewhere along the path it occurs to me that Jesus probably had the mother-of-all-headaches when he was carrying his cross. The thought gives me some ambivalent consolation.

Traveling at speed, within an hour I am sweating and puffing. My legs and temples ache, but I can see the end in sight and catch glimpses of the enormous concrete cross as I round the bends in the trail. By now, I sincerely regret not having packed a water bottle, and I'm pretty sure the bread-and-water fast was a very foolish idea.

I reach the station where *Jesus Is Taken Down from the Cross*, and—my headache disappears.

This headache has been such an intense pain that I am instantly aware when it is gone. Amazed by this, I walk up close to the plaque and stare at the limp figure of Jesus with nail holes in his hands and feet.

The pain is over.

Not only the pain in my head but all his pain is over too. He is dead.

I turn away and scramble up the path. I put my fingers to my temples and press to see if the headache is really gone. It seems to have vanished for no reason.

That's weird.

I pause at the station that shows Jesus being laid in the tomb, and I say the prayers. This is the last station. Well, except for that new one about the Resurrection, but I am going to skip that. It interrupts the thread of the meditation, so I have already decided I will avert my eyes and walk right past it.

I turn the bend in the path, and the Resurrection plaque shines into my eyes like all the others, but instead of walking up close, I push on up the hill.

Then—at that precise moment—I am struck with the most intense feeling of joy. I have never experienced anything like this before. Somewhere within my heart and lungs and bones there is a welling of extreme emotional lightness.

I stop.

I swivel around on the narrow path and swing my gaze behind me to the station I have just rushed past. I can feel an involuntary smile in my eyes and on my lips as I reverse direction and go back the way I have come. There are people praying, so I maneuver my way among them and stare up at the image of the risen Christ. The overwhelming feeling of joy intensifies. And it is so overwhelming I can't stand still.

I take off again, up the mountain. When I reach the concrete cross, I go up and touch it.

It feels like concrete.

I look around at the other pilgrims. There are about twenty people standing about, snapping photos, and catching their breath. I blurt out "Good afternoon!" first in English, and when that prompts only small grins, I announce it in Spanish, and then Croatian.

They smile back, shake their heads, point at themselves, and say, "Filipino."

I shake their hands enthusiastically, babbling at them unintelligibly in three different languages. They laugh at my exuberance and my uninhibited friendliness, and so do I. This irrational giddiness is amusing even to me.

After I have become best friends with nearly everyone on top of Mount Krizevac, I dart down the path as fast as I can leap from rock to rock without actually tumbling headfirst down the mountain. At the bottom I meet one of my fellow pilgrims from Kalamazoo and talk her into sharing supper with me at the restaurant. The whole fasting idea has completely vanished from my mind. We laugh and tell stories from the week and are soon joined by some of our fellow pilgrims for a jubilant evening of conversation, wine, beer, and Dubrovnik pizza.

We leave Medjugorje the next day. The feeling of joy stays with me through sitting outside of Split in a six-hour traffic jam caused by the visit of Pope John Paul II; it persists when I am faced with a cancelled connecting flight in Washington, DC; and I crack up laughing when, due to a snowstorm, we end up in the Pittsburgh airport instead of Chicago.

I attempt to stifle down the giggles when one of my traveling companions breaks into tears from the combined stress of being awake for twenty-six hours and losing her luggage. Ruth, the lady who was able to look directly into the setting sun, catches sight of me with my lips sucked inward, and irrational humor bubbles inside her, too. We sneak off to find a café where we can together release the hilarity of being stranded in Pittsburgh.

This extreme emotional high lasts for three weeks. Back, finally, in Kalamazoo, I tell exuberant stories about my pilgrimage to scores of indulgent friends and relatives and show the photos over and over again. I give away medals and rosaries and fistfuls of holy cards.

Then I wake up one morning with a head cold, and everything goes back to normal.

27

FRIENDS OF THE POOR

It is our duty to prefer the service of the poor to everything else and to offer such service as quickly as possible. If a needy person requires medicine or other help during prayer time, do whatever has to be done with peace of mind. Offer the deed to God as your prayer.

—ST. VINCENT DE PAUL

We Vincentians call ourselves "Friends of the Poor." Our goal is to change ourselves into friends of Christ, and since we know Christ is in the poor, we are trying to do this by being their friends.

Becoming a true friend requires a lot of emotional energy from me. I am not the most social person out there. I studied math in college. After that, I taught math; thus, I have been a geek for many years. Too many conversations in my life have gone like this:

"Hi, I'm Jane."

"Nice to meet you, Jane. My name's Sam. What do you do for a living?"

"I teach math."

"Oh. Really? I hate math. Absolutely my worst subject."

I never know what to say at this point, so the conversation peters out miserably.

But my visit to Medjugorje has taught me I can't hide behind my geekiness any longer. I now know there are lots and lots of people climbing the mountain with me and I need to offer an outstretched hand. Mountains should not be scaled alone in silent meditation. The joy at the top reaches out to the other pilgrims because joy is neither frivolous nor solitary—it needs to be shared.

One of the great things about being a volunteer at a thrift store is that no one asks me what I do for living. I have made wonderful friends among the other volunteers and also among some of the donors. But becoming a friend of the people we help—that's kind of like being a math teacher. The balance of power is so skewed that it is an immediate barrier to friendship. I am the seemingly rich person giving the money away, and they are the seemingly needy people asking for help. This is not a good basis for friendship. This is like climbing the mountain solo. Maybe this is why our patron, St. Vincent, tells us to help as quickly as possible, to drop everything, even our rosary beads, when someone asks for our assistance. Our quick response is a sign of our sincere concern for them, and it takes some of the power out of our hands and puts it in theirs. If we delay our help to fit our own schedule, we control not only the money but also their time and add to their anxiety.

The people seeking help at St. Vincent de Paul are among the most patient, long-suffering souls I have ever known. They wait in lines wherever they go—taking the bus, applying for assistance, and getting medical care in emergency rooms. There is no such thing as online banking or an ATM when every bill must be paid with a money order. The poor in this world are in the "cash only" lines, and those lines are long.

One day I am talking with a woman who has been displaced by Hurricane Katrina. She has moved her family to Michigan because they have relatives here and a place to stay, but that doesn't mean there are jobs here, too. The strain shows on her face when she says, "I'm going to tell you something: Americans don't know how to starve to death. It's just not in our nature. Americans aren't going to sit down under a tree with their baby in their lap and watch it die. Our ancestors weren't the kind to do that, which is why they came here in the first place, and we aren't either. If we can't get help when we need it, Americans will take action, even if it's desperate action."

St. Vincent's advice to "offer service as quickly as possible" rings in my ears, but I still refuse to hear it in a ringing telephone.

Late in the evening, Rita leaves a message on my answering machine to call her. I have helped her financially with quite a lot of small things lately, and I am feeling a teensy bit put-upon. I put off returning her call until the next morning.

When I finally get back with her, I hear a sigh in her voice. She has broken her ankle.

"Oh, no! How bad is it?"

She isn't sure. At first she waited to see if it would get better, but after three days, it swelled up, so she talked a friend into giving her a ride to the hospital. The doctors x-rayed it and found some bone spurs, considerable swelling, and "inconclusive" stuff, so they decided to put a split cast on it.

"They wanted to cut my jeans at the ankle," she complains. "But I wasn't going to let them ruin my only good ones, so I took the jeans off instead, and they gave me some of those paper pants to wear. They wrapped the whole thing up big and bulky and gave me a pair of crutches and said I could go home, but my ride had left hours ago."

I wince because that was probably when she had left the message for me. "Did you call a cab?"

"I didn't have any money with me, so I asked the hospital people if they would pay for one, but they said they don't do that no more. The lady handed me some bus tokens, but I said, 'There's no buses running this late at night.' But she just pushed my wheelchair to the front entrance and left me there anyway."

"Nice."

"I got the sciatica in one leg, a cast on the other foot, two crutches and a cane—and I'm sitting out on the sidewalk *wearing paper pants*." She laughs. "I tell you, Jane, hospital people are strange folk."

The conclusion of the story was that she called her neighbor, who doesn't own a car but her son does. After he got off work, the son collected Rita from in front of the hospital and transported her home.

I tell Rita how sorry I am that another burden has fallen on her, and I apologize for not returning her phone call earlier. She is not overly concerned about any of the past twenty-four hours, but she wonders if I might be able to drive her to a follow-up appointment the next day at the community health clinic. We arrange that, and I ask her if she received the birthday card I sent. She tells me what a lovely birthday she had and how good everyone was to her.

"What did you do?" I ask, thinking in my middle-class brain that everyone does *something* on their birthday.

"Why, I sat in the yard nearly all day. It was perfect weather. My neighbor grilled some chicken and some of the folks across the street brought over some beer. I don't drink anymore, and everybody around here knows that, but they asked my permission if it was all right that they shared the beer around, and I said it was. Wasn't that nice of them to ask me like that? It was because it was my birthday. I have real good neighbors."

"That sounds like . . . a good time," I say.

"It was. I love sitting in the yard with all the people around, just as long as nobody gets acting loony. Beer will do that, you know. But the people behaved this time. I had a real nice day. I didn't twist my ankle until the next week."

We continue chatting, and I mention that the police caught the guy who used my credit cards.

"Good," she says. "People who steal are a curse on this earth. Did they pick him up?"

"Yeah. They caught him on security cameras at the stores, so eventually he pleaded guilty. I'm glad I didn't have to go to court."

"How long did he get?"

"I don't know. I don't think he's been sentenced yet."

I ask her if she has heard anything about her application for disability. Her lawyer succeeded in getting her a hearing five months ago, and she was awarded the disability by the judge, but the actual date when the checks will start coming has been pushed off into the future again and again. For once, she has some good news to tell me.

"My worker says they can't send my checks to my house—everything has to be direct deposit into a bank account. I don't have a bank account, so I walked to the one down the street, but they won't open an account unless I have at least twenty dollars to start it. I took that money you gave me last time for the Laundromat, and the money my sister sent me for my birthday, and now I've got things all set and ready to go as soon as they decide to release the disability money."

"That's great news," I tell her. "How much will you get each month?"

"Six hundred thirty-four dollars. Of course, when it starts they will be cutting my food stamps from one hundred fifty to sixteen dollars, and my rent goes up from zero to two hundred eighty-seven."

I do some quick math in my head. "So you'll have three hundred forty-seven dollars per month to pay for your phone, utilities, groceries, laundry, transportation, clothing, and anything else you need."

"Yes," she nods in satisfaction. "And the first thing I'm going to buy is a new bed."

I chew on my lip.

"I've never had a brand new mattress before. How much does a new one cost, Jane? You got any idea?"

28

LEAVING AHEAD, PART 2

Customers in the thrift shop often ask us about Dorothy.

After her hip heals and she is released from "assisted living," she comes back to work for several months. Her family doesn't want her to drive anymore, so one or another of her children or grandchildren drop her off and pick her up every time. This works okay for a while, but eventually, after some weeks of this routine, another health crisis occurs, and she goes back to the senior care facility.

Now when our customers inquire about "that sweet little white-haired cashier," I ask for prayers for her, and they generously provide them, sometimes on the spot. We put a word in with the Virgin Mary for her at our monthly St. Vincent de Paul meetings and during our daily group prayer times, too.

I visit her occasionally, but she doesn't always know who I am. When I go to see her, I don't give her the Serenity Prayer. Instead, I bring her a bouquet of yellow flowers because I think she likes yellow. She would never tell me if she didn't, so I am only guessing.

I don't like to visit people in hospitals and nursing homes. It feels awkward to me to carry on a conversation with someone who is wearing their pajamas while I am fully dressed. This is a personal quirk that doesn't seem to go away, no matter how hard I try to ignore it or pretend it doesn't matter. I really admire people who work or volunteer in nursing homes and hospitals. I could not do what they do.

People occasionally say to me, "Jane, I don't know how you can volunteer in that thrift store with the drunks and the addicts and the street people coming in there every day."

Well.

Our customers may be loud, or zoned, or smelly, but they are usually wearing regular clothes, and if they aren't, we find some for them. And people at the thrift store know where they are. And if they don't *like* where they are, they can leave the place and never come back.

On the other hand, pajama-clad captivity is difficult for me.

I think it is difficult for Dorothy, too. When I visit, she prefers to be dressed in her Talbot Petite fashions, even if she is just snoozing in a wheelchair. On the occasions when I find her in bed, dressed in a nightgown, she is embarrassed and confused, which is hard on both of us. Lately, this happens more often than not.

One day I walk into her room, and she is wide awake, sitting up and wearing a pink cardigan. I lean down and peck her on the cheek, pat her hand, and say, "How are you today, Dorothy?"

She smiles at me and says, "I'm just fine, Jane. How are things at the store?"

I am amazed. She didn't know me from Adam the last time I saw her. I sit down in a chair and she asks about my two daughters and Dean's business. We talk about the health of the other volunteers at St. Vinnie's and how sales have been this year. We are both fully dressed and fully awake and it's almost like old times.

After our visit, when I stand to leave and bid her good-bye, she squeezes my hand in hers, and she says, "I love you, Jane."

My eyes well-up. We have known each other for nearly thirteen years, but we have never said this to each other. We talk about the store, our families, how best to help the poor and how the poor have helped us, and even about God occasionally, but not about how much we mean to each other. "I love you, too, Dorothy," I tell her, and I give her a gentle embrace.

Two weeks later I hear the news that Dorothy went on ahead.

They hold her funeral in the cathedral of St. Augustine, the church we can see from St. Vinnie's. She ironed the linens and arranged the flowers in that place for years, so it is nice to see it all decorated for her for once.

A few weeks later I am working at the store when her daughter drops off some boxes of donations. In one of them I find a small silver ring that fits my pinkie, so I ask the other volunteers to price it for me so I can buy it.

After we die, someone else has to clean out our house.

This, too, is a gift. If we accept it.

29

AT PEACE WITH THE PRIESTS

During his time in office, the Most Reverend Paul Vincent Donovan, the first bishop of the Diocese of Kalamazoo, was a consistent supporter of our efforts to assist the poor. He would occasionally visit during our store business hours, he had an open door for our leaders, and every year on our feast day he would celebrate with all the Vincentians from the diocese by holding a Mass at the cathedral and afterward sharing dinner with us.

But there was one point in our history when he stepped in and rearranged the leadership of our St. Vincent de Paul group. This was necessary because we had gone off track and become so focused on running the thrift store that we were neglecting helping the poor. It was a dark time for our little community and a dark time in our relationship with the hierarchy of the diocese.

There were grumblings among us: *If the bishop doesn't like the way we are doing things, then maybe he should do them himself.*

It was around this time that I first picked up and read *The Rule of St. Benedict*, the classic, sixth-century instructions on how to live in a community. This one-hundred-page manual gives details for everything needed to run a religious organization, from sharing the labor to making time for prayer to electing leaders and to correcting the wayward. The point that interests me most about St. Benedict's advice is that he gives serious warning to the problem of "murmuring." At first I don't catch on to what exactly he means by this, but gradually it becomes clear that murmuring encompasses all the griping, gossiping, and critical comments that seep into human conversations everywhere.

Murmuring is the medieval equivalent of anything from cattiness to a rant.

To St. Benedict, murmuring spells the sure death of a community. A negative stream of complaints, no matter how justified, is the opposite of a loving relationship and will kill the relationship eventually.

This is not to say that St. Benedict thinks problems should be swept under the rug. He advocates an uncomplicated system:

"As often as anything important is to be done . . . the prioress or abbot shall call the whole community together and explain . . . and after hearing the advice of the members, let them ponder it and follow what they judge the wiser course. . . the Spirit often reveals what is better to the younger. The community members . . . are to express their opinions in all humility and not presume to defend their own views obstinately. The decision is the prioress's or abbot's to make . . . to settle everything with foresight and fairness."

Sounds like the way Dorothy would handle things.

Back to Bishop Donovan.

After the crackdown from the bishop, eventually our little St. Vincent de Paul group pulled itself together. We reexamined the methods we were using to assist the poor, we began to pray more regularly, and we got a grip on some of our complaining.

We are still far from being a perfect community, as this book shows, but we care enough about it to keep working at changing ourselves.

At the thrift store, the part of our Rule that helps keep us on track is remembering what St. Vincent de Paul said: "The poor are our masters, and it is no exaggeration to call them this, because Our Lord is in the poor." As long as we focus on this, and put aside our murmurings, we are not as apt to stray far off the path of helping the needy and learning from them. The bishops and the priests are part of this community too. Figuring out their role in our lives is as much our job as it is theirs. Murmuring about their role sometimes impedes our way.

When Bishop Donovan is finally allowed to retire, the St. Vincent de Paul Thrift Store is the recipient of several bags of black dress slacks and suit jackets. Our customers are delighted, and we are grateful for the donation.

He doesn't give us any of those unique Roman-collared shirts, though.

Even after Bishop Donovan's retirement we continue to see him occasionally at the store. He never makes a production out of his visits. He walks in, hands over a bag of donations, glances around and compliments something about the place, then leaves.

Watching him go, we look at each other and say, "Wait. Wasn't that—?"

One Saturday, our crew of furniture haulers, consisting of my husband, Dean, and two Hackett Catholic Central students, go to an address at The Fountains, a retirement community. They are instructed to pick up a couch that will be in one of the parking structures on the premises, but first they need to stop at the reception desk. When they arrive, the receptionist tells them where to go and picks up her phone to notify someone to meet them there.

At the garage our crew is surprised to find a man wearing a Roman collar and casual slacks waiting for them. Dean knows who he is and introduces him to the others, and Bishop Donovan is delighted to meet the students. It isn't his couch, but he has been instrumental in directing the donor (one of his neighbors) to give it to the St. Vincent de Paul Society.

Before the students bend down to grab hold and lift it onto the truck, the bishop pulls a small bottle of holy water from his pocket and blesses the couch thoroughly. He explains to the crew that by blessing the couch, he hopes to bless whoever will be receiving it.

Our high school students have never had their volunteer work treated in quite this way before, and surprise shows on their faces. When he is done with the sofa, Bishop Donovan smiles warmly at them, shakes hands again, and then—he sprinkles holy water on the grinning crew, too.

It is a blessing well given, and it is well received.

The hierarchy, in the form of this humble bishop, has given a priestly blessing to the humble work that God has called the laity to do. And this gift, only partially understood, has been accepted.

Isn't this all we really need from each other?

In a community we are each gifts to one another. The rich, with their resources, are a gift to the poor. And the poor, with their hard-earned wisdom, are a gift to the rich.

The priests and bishops are a gift to the faithful, but if the faithful did not exist, there would be no need for priests and bishops. We are all pilgrims from many places climbing a rocky hill together. And this jumble of a community is the greatest gift of all.

But only if the gift is accepted.

This is our choice, and sometimes it is not a clear choice at all. Sometimes the community looks oddly fuzzy, multicolored, and useless to us, and we hesitate to open the lid. And if we take the chance, we may discover that we are all pieces of string too small to save.

But God saves us anyway.

QUESTIONS FOR DISCUSSION

1. The author says that her stories are like pieces of string too small to save. And yet, strung together, they have meaning. What was your favorite bit of string in this book, and what did you like about it?

2. Jane Knuth is a teacher by profession, and any teacher worthy of the name is also a learner. The St. Vincent De Paul workers are instructed to see their clients, or customers, as their teachers, who provide good lessons. Is there a particular lesson that Jane learned that you also find valuable?

3. Have you thought about how your "things" will be dispersed or disposed of when you no longer need them? How will you feel when someone else makes those decisions for you?

4. At Medjugorje, Mary tells the visionaries and pilgrims to pray for young people. The young people in this book are important figures. What do you think the author is communicating about people like Jeremy, the refrigerator mover? Are there young people in your

life who are seeking purpose and meaning and who need your prayers?

5. The Medjugorje experience is interwoven with the thrift-store vignettes. Look at how one story ends and the next begins. What connections were you able to see between these two different worlds the author presented? Share an example.

6. Likewise, the story of the theft of Jane's wallet is a thread through the book. What are some of the questions and lessons that this story raises?

7. Unlike people with resources, when the poor become victims of crime, they face many difficulties in obtaining justice. What are some examples of these difficulties from the stories in the book or from your own experience?

8. Have you ever been a victim of a crime, and if so, how did you handle it? Did justice and/or forgiveness follow?

9. Jane's painting instructor, Ken, tells her she will not succeed with painting until she experiences joy. How does this apply to the spiritual life?

10. A fellow thrift-store volunteer asks Jane how she knows if one of their customers is telling the truth. She responds by telling stories of two women, one

whose explanation of her children's different surnames rings true, and the other whose story of needing help seems suspicious. Jane's answer to the volunteer is somewhat ambiguous. Could you handle working in a thrift store knowing that sometimes the truth isn't being told?

11. At a mass in Medjugorje, Jane learns that Mary has asked us to pray for priests, but Jane has doubts that they need our prayers. Later, back at the thrift store, she and co-volunteer Shirley (who has admirably out-fitted an odoriferous homeless man) discuss the stench of the actions of child-abusing priests. How does Jane finally come to understand what Mary is asking with this request to pray for priests?

12. Does God want only rich children to have ice cream? Why or why not, in your opinion?

13. It seems that God wanted Jane to be in Medjugorje even though she initially had objections to making the trip. Jane says that she has long been drawn to mys-tics, though she did not see herself as a mystic. Yet she did receive several gifts, understandings, or intense experiences there. Which ones seemed most signific-ant to you?

14. Would you consider a pilgrimage to Medjugorje after reading about Jane's experience there?

15. One conclusion Jane draws from Medjugorje is that God likes groups. How does this change her outlook?

16. The user of Jane's credit cards is identified as Otis, a person whom Jane has helped and who has given Jane several material gifts. On the same day she learns this, she knows Otis has an appointment to choose Christmas gifts for his children. Jane is faced with an uncomfortable dilemma about what to do when she sees him. She goes to the nearby cathedral to pray for guidance, but God doesn't seem to answer. Eventually an answer does evolve. What is it?

17. Jane reflects on trying to be a friend of the poor, as St. Vincent De Paul instructed. The balance of power in such a relationship lies with the giver, not the recipient. What are some ways to make the balance fairer and thus allow friendship to develop?

18. The author says that a gift is a gift only if it is accepted. What do you think that means? What are some nonmaterial gifts you have received and accepted lately?

ACKNOWLEDGMENTS

I am grateful for my teachers, namely everyone whose story is told in these pages. I have disguised some of the people, but many generous souls agreed to let me use their names.

Jeremy, from chapter 10, was one of the first people I contacted. After reading the chapter, he wrote back to me by e-mail:

> You certainly captured what I remember most about that day—touring the facility. I grew up in the shadow of the paper mill, and I can even remember plotting with my brothers to sneak out late at night to discover the hidden treasures of the building. We never did, of course, but half the fun was in planning the adventure. As such, when I was contacted to pick up refrigerators, I jumped at the opportunity.
>
> I remember a feeling of uneasiness while I was there; mainly my own. I knew those men were losing their jobs, and I didn't want to do anything to remind them of that. It was considerate of them to think of donating the refrigerators amidst their anxiety. Your depiction of me is spot-on: a boy, nervous around grown men (from lack of a male role model), with his head down and hands in pockets.

Still though, my curiosity and excitement could not be contained.

The place was a maze. I remember big open spaces and a lot of steel parts. I imagined being a piece of paper traveling quickly through the facility, or strapping on some roller skates and blazing across the lengthy, smooth surface of fresh paper. I was captivated.

On a side note, that man-starved boy appreciated the little time he spent with your husband. The small moments I've spent with good and honest men lsike your husband have shaped me into the man I am and always aspire to be. Please thank him for me, and thank you for seeing the blessings in small everyday events!

(After reading this, I asked Jeremy if he ever thought of writing professionally!)

I am grateful to all the members of the Society of St. Vincent de Paul with whom I have worked over the last sixteen years. Dorothy, Mary, Alice, Bernie D., Gene, Walter, Jim H., Frank, Cheryl, and Deacon Bob are all people I have looked to for advice and wisdom innumerable times. They have been persevering leaders. Jane C., Peggy, Dottie, Fran, Mary Kay, Pat, Mike, Joan M., Kim, Joan S., Michelle N., Chris, Chuck, Lara, Jim W., and Jane H. are the members of the Friday crew I work with every week. They are the workday spiritual guides God has given me. Each one of them is truly a gift and a grace in every sense of these words. The rest of the community at

St. Vinnie's is part of God's gift, too. They are Bonnie, Margaret, Nancee, Marilyn, Jenny, Mona, Mary H., Fred, Kathleen, Lois, Bob, Lyndi, Judy, Gene R., Kathy, Barb, Janice, Betty, Roz, Jerry, Sally, Elaine, Jim Heeter, Matt, Rosalie, Paula, Gloria, Helene, Gerry, Nora, Sue, Geraldine, Pam, Nathan, Sister Ann Carolyn, Argie, Sheila, Kelli, Laura, Brad, and Steve.

Martha D. persuaded me to go to Medjugorje, for which I am in her debt forever. Tom G. shared his Bosnian adventures with me, and his astounding faith with his students, who included my two daughters. Mr. Ken is a gifted teacher of both art and spirituality.

Rita is still teaching me how to be "a friend of the poor." I am a slow learner, but she is endlessly patient. I am grateful that she allowed me to tell her story of the day-to-day trials of being financially stressed in our society.

Dorothy, Shirley, and Bishop Donovan have all gone on ahead. The multiplicity of blessings I received from each of them continues to expand throughout the world. Goodness is like that.

Whenever I get the opportunity, I tell people about the generosity and expertise of the staff at Loyola Press. Steve Connor, Joe Durepos, and Vinita Hampton Wright talked me through the writing, while Bret Nicholaus, Sharon Roth, Rosemary Zalewski, Rosemary Lane, Denise Gorss, Ray Ives, and Andrew Yankech coached me through the rest of what it takes to publish a book. They are all patient teachers, and I am their grateful student.

My writing group, Bess, Gretchen, Katie, Kathy, Joyce, Ginny, Sheila, Kristin, Krissa, and Pearline, are also spiritual companions. They are the ones who help me put into words the wonders God has put into my hands.

A special thank-you to Sue Andrews for writing the discussion questions. Every author needs readers like her!

My mom, Dottie, and my mother-in-law, Lorraine, always give me encouragement beyond price. They also buy a lot of my books! Their love and support are perfect in every way.

My husband, Dean, and daughters, Ellen and Martha, are God's grace, gifts, and love that I can hold in my hands and heart. The only woman in the history of the world who has a more wonderful family is the Blessed Virgin Mary, and she doesn't count.

Also by Jane Knuth

Thrift Store Saints
Meeting Jesus 25¢ at a Time

$13.95 • Pb • 3301-2

Thrift Store Saints is a collection of true stories based on Jane Knuth's experiences serving the poor at a St. Vincent de Paul thrift store in the inner city of Kalamazoo, Michigan. Knuth learns that when we serve the poor, they end up helping us as much as we help them. Throughout the book we are introduced to new "saints," as Knuth thoughtfully, at times humorously, describes how her encounters with the poorest people led her to the greatest riches of God's grace.

Also Available

Radical Compassion
Finding Christ in the Heart of the Poor

Gary Smith, SJ

$17.95 • Pb • 2000-5

For more than 25 years, Gary Smith, SJ, has been helping the poor as he lives among them and ministers to their needs. In *Radical Compassion*, Smith chronicles his life and work in the poverty-stricken Old Town section of Portland, Oregon. These touching and often heart-breaking stories reveal the problems and issues facing the growing homeless population in our country. As we witness Smith helping the poor, we learn the lessons of love, forgiveness, and acceptance that have radically changed his heart—and can radically change ours as well.

To order: call 800-621-1008,
visit www.loyolapress.com/store,
or visit your local bookseller.

Also Available

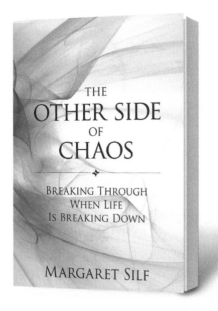

The Other Side of Chaos
Breaking Through When Life Is
Breaking Down

Margaret Silf

$13.95 • Pb • 3308-1

In *The Other Side of Chaos*, best-selling author Margaret Silf looks closely at the subject of chaos—and the intrinsic transition it brings—through the lens of Christian spirituality. Through Scripture stories and verses, personal accounts, and other anecdotes, Silf helps us develop an authentic "spirituality of transition" that leads us to live out life's changes constructively, creatively, and confidently.

Also Available

Saints at Heart
How Fault-Filled,
Problem-Prone,
Imperfect People like Us
Can Be Holy

Bert Ghezzi

$12.95 • Pb • 3544-3

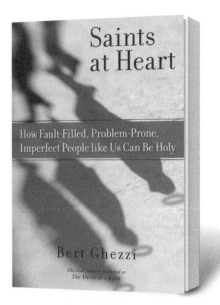

Best-selling author Bert
Ghezzi believes every one
of us can be holy, and he
shows us how in *Saints at
Heart*. By pointing out that
all the saints—even the
apostles—were sinners, he helps us understand how holiness
is not about being perfect, but rather about making a heartfelt
decision to fall in love with God and put God first. Fittingly,
each of the 10 saints featured in this book illustrates a specific
spiritual practice that can help us draw closer to God.

To order: call 800-621-1008,
visit www.loyolapress.com/store,
or visit your local bookseller.